Patrol Procedures for Private Security Professionals

Douglas W. Henrich, B.Sc., CPP

Conestoga College of Applied Arts and Technology

Toronto

I wish to dedicate this book to my mother, Dorothy Gertrude Barriball, who has given me more than she realizes, and to the memory of my brother, Gary Carson Henrich.

Canadian Cataloguing in Publication Data

Henrich, Douglas W., 1958–
    Patrol procedures for private security professionals

Includes bibliographical references and index.
ISBN 0-13-029145-5

1. Police, Private–Canada. 2. Private security services–Canada. I. Title.

HV8099.C3H46 2001   363.28'9'0971   C00-932515-8

ISBN 0-13-029145-5

Vice President, Editorial Director: Michael Young
Senior Editor: Sophia Fortier
Signing Representative: Stephen Lemieux
Associate Editor: Susan Ratkaj
Production Editor: Sherry Torchinsky
Copy Editor: Claudia Forgas
Production Coordinator: Wendy Moran
Page Layout: Gerry Dunn
Art Director: Mary Opper
Cover Design: Sarah Battersby
Cover Image: Photo Disc
4 5 6 DPC 08 07 06

Printed and bound in Canada.

CONTENTS

PREFACE

In December 1999, I was asked by Don Douglas, program co-ordinator for Law and Security Administration and Police Foundations at Conestoga College in Kitchener, Ontario, to instruct a second-year Law and Security Administration course called Patrol Procedures. While developing the course outline, I could not find any current Canadian or American textbooks that specifically addressed patrol procedures for the security professional. A review of the literature revealed many books that included components on patrol procedures within the broader context of security, but none that specifically focused on the practical aspects of this subject.

Patrol Procedures for Private Security Professionals has been developed for the practising security professional or for anyone who wishes to learn about security patrol practices. Portions of this text (Chapter 11, Order Maintenance Patrols; Chapter 13, Bomb Threats; Chapter 15, Crime Scene Preservation; and Chapter 18, Assisting Emotionally Disturbed Persons) may appear to cover material that goes beyond the required duties of a regular Security Patrol Officer and, indeed, may lie within the Security Manager or Security Director's responsibilities. Such material was included because it is vital for all security professionals to have a basic understanding of these topics. Security personnel are expected to be prepared to deal with various critical issues that affect the areas under their protection.

I am not writing for the stereotypical "Security Guard" who only has to focus on very limited duties as outlined within his or her post orders. My intended audience is the true security professional who wants to consistently deliver the highest quality of service to employers and clients in the safest manner possible.

You will find a lot of material related to officer safety throughout this textbook. At times it may seem somewhat repetitive. This is such an important topic, however, that I have provided practical examples as to how it can be related to all aspects of a Security Officer's patrol function. All too often, Security Officers are not provided any formal training on officer safety, nor do their post orders focus on such issues. Since Security Officers, for the most part, lack Police Officers' extensive training, equipment, and back up resources, it is very important that they be aware of officer safety issues.

This book is a learning resource and should be used to supplement any existing training programs or documented policies and procedures that you may be required to follow in your specific occupation. It provides an introduction to the fundamental aspects of patrol procedures that security professionals may encounter during their security career. While arrest procedures, legal aspects of security, and defensive tactics are beyond the scope of this text, references to these topics are provided at the end of this textbook.

ACKNOWLEDGMENTS

I wish to acknowledge the following individuals for the assistance and support they provided to me in the writing of this textbook:

Don Douglas: Co-ordinator, Law and Security Administration and Police Foundations, Conestoga College, for giving me the opportunity to develop this textbook.

Mike Fenton: Director of Consulting and Support Services, Intercon Security Ltd., and Certified Protection Professional (CPP), for sharing with me his depth of security knowledge and experience as a Crime Prevention Through Environmental Design (CPTED) practitioner.

Gordon Hurley: Law enforcement trainer and experiential educator, for suggesting reference material and for providing valuable suggestions on how to improve this textbook.

Ed Nowicki: Author and law enforcement trainer, for the written and video material that he forwarded to me.

Students: All the second year Law and Security Administration students at Conestoga College who attended my Patrol Procedures course from January to April 2000.

I would also like to acknowledge Peel Regional Police, Conestoga College, and Intercon Security. This book would not have been possible without the insight I gained while serving as a Police Officer with Peel Regional Police. In particular, I wish to thank Cst. Tom McKay, Peel Regional Police Service, Crime Prevention Services, for first introducing me to CPTED. As well, Conestoga College has been very generous in allowing the publisher to use the instructor's manual I developed for the Patrol Procedures course. I also acknowledge the depth of security experience that I gained throughout my career with Intercon Security. In particular, I wish to thank managers John Byrnes, John Ranger, and Max Warmuth for their support and encouragement throughout my career with the company.

Where possible, I have acknowledged all sources and references used to develop this textbook. If I have omitted any, I apologize in advance.

Any errors, omissions or inaccuracies are solely the responsibility of myself.

Douglas Henrich, B.Sc., CPP
Toronto, Ontario

HOW TO USE THIS TEXTBOOK

This textbook was written as a reference book for students completing law and security programs, for current security practitioners who wish to review their understanding of patrol procedures, and for the general public who wish to understand how private Security Officers conduct security patrols. If this textbook is used in a classroom setting, the text is intended to be supplemented by training videos, in-class lectures, discussion, and practical role playing. As this text provides a general overview of patrol procedures, students are encouraged to review the bibliography to seek out more specialized resources.

Questions have been included at the end of each chapter to assist the student in understanding and applying the security principles reviewed. The questions are categorized into three levels: A, B, and C. Level A questions are short answer questions with the answers found directly in the textbook. Level B are more application-oriented and may require further detail to answer completely. Level C questions require thoughtful analysis and review of material presented within the chapter. The framework to answer Level C questions has been provided within the chapter but not all of the required information will be found in the chapter.

An instructor's manual (ISBN: 0-13-029144-7) is available for instructors who require greater information on how to use this textbook in a course.

Every effort has been made to ensure *Patrol Procedures for Private Security Professionals* reflects the best current practices prevalent in the industry. However, opinions on best practices differ and students must follow the directions and policies of whatever organization they belong to.

ABOUT THE AUTHOR

Douglas Henrich has been a member of the security industry for over twenty years and has also served as a Police Constable with the Peel Regional Police. Doug began his Security career in 1976 as a Security Officer with Intercon Security and has progressed through a variety of positions within Intercon including: Security Officer, Shift Supervisor, Site Supervisor, Mobile Supervisor, Account Director, and Recruitment Officer. He gained extensive field experience providing security to retail, commercial, industrial, residential and institutional accounts.

In his present role as Intercon's ISO 9000 Coordinator, Doug assisted in the design and implementation of the procedures that guided Intercon Security's Toronto Branch towards ISO 9002 certification. For the last three years, Doug has also been cross-training as a Security Consultant and has worked independently on several consulting assignments. Doug serves as the Vice-Chair for the Law and Security Administration and Police Foundations Program Advisory Committee at Conestoga College and instructs part-time within the Law and Security Administration Program there.

Doug is a current member of the Canadian Association for Security and Intelligence Studies, the Ontario Association of Police Educators, the American Society for Industrial Security, the American Society of Law Enforcement Trainers, the International CPTED Association and a past member of the Ontario Roadrunners Association.

Doug has received certification as an ISO 9000 Lead Auditor, a Use of Force Theory Instructor and as a Level 1 CPTED Practitioner. Doug also holds a Bachelor of Science Degree in mathematics from the University of Toronto and has received his Certified Protection Professional (CPP) designation through the American Society for Industrial Security.

Outside of Security, Doug is the owner of D. Henrich Tutoring and has worked as an Educational Consultant for over twenty years.

HISTORY OF PRIVATE SECURITY

LEARNING OUTCOMES

At the conclusion of this chapter, you will be able to

- Trace the development of private security from ancient to modern times
- Identify early security firms that were formed in the United States
- Identify the licencing requirements for contract Security Officers in Canada

SECURITY FROM ANCIENT TO MODERN TIMES

The Code of Hamurabi (circa 1700 BC) was the first recorded body of laws regulating trade, commerce, agriculture and all of the professions. Penalties for violations were severe and included flogging, impaling, exposure to wild beasts, burning, slavery, and crucifixion.[1] Under the code, criminals would often be branded or mutilated to alert the population to their criminal nature and to act as a general deterrent.

Greek States

The early Greek states were the first to establish a professional security force to protect life, limb, and property. This means that private security is older than public law enforcement by at least 1500 years.[2]

The Roman Empire

Under Caesar Augustus, the Praetorian Guard was established almost 2000 years ago. It comprised two distinct segments: urban cohorts that maintained security within the city; and vigiles (vigilantes), a secret police agency that protected state security.

Britain

Civilians On Patrol

After the fall of the Roman Empire, many citizens of Rome fled to the British Isles. They settled in *tuns* or "early towns."[3] Tuns laws were enforced separately by what was each town's forerunner of the modern municipal police department. Under English Common Law (prior to AD 1066) every able-bodied man was obliged to join in communal pursuit of offenders.[4] This law may have inspired the origin of the word *cop* or "civilian on patrol." The obligation to join in communal pursuit of offenders forms the basis of "citizen's arrest" and remains the only arrest authority of private security personnel. It also forms the basis of the existing Criminal Code of Canada requirement that everyone, without reasonable excuse, is required on request to assist a Peace Officer or Police Officer in the performance of his or her duties.[5]

There were no prisons in feudal England, nor was there a death penalty. Crimes were perceived as being directly against the person. Retribution was an individual rather than a collective act.[6]

Norman Law-Enforcement Reforms

In 1066 the conquest of England by William, Duke of Normandy, transformed crime from being an offence against the individual to being an offence against the state. The Normans introduced a circuit judge system and generated major reforms in law enforcement techniques. In 1116 the Laws of Henry established a grand jury system and distinguished between a felony (serious offence) and a misdemeanour (less serious offence).[7] These distinctions compare with indictable and summary conviction offences in the Canadian system.

The Magna Carta and Individual Rights

In 1215 the signing of the Magna Carta established due process and a system to protect the rights of the individual.[8] Prior to 1215 there was no inherent system that recognized the rights of the individual. People did not have any "natural rights," but had only the rights that were conferred to them as a result of their position in the community. It would take the advent of the Industrial Revolution before the same rights would be bestowed on women, however.

Specialized Police Agencies of the Renaissance

As commerce and trade prospered, a strong merchant class emerged. Their demand for protection fostered the development of early police agencies. By 1500 there were six types of police agencies operating in Britain:

1. *Merchant Police.* Private security hired to guard buildings.
2. *Parochial Police.* Officers who protected people and property within a parish (a religious division within a city).
3. *Watches and Wards.* Civilian patrols similar to neighbourhood watches.
4. *Bow Street Runners.* Special investigators.
5. *Thames River Police.* Special police appointed to patrol the Thames River and area.
6. *Special Constables.* Officers assigned to a specific jurisdiction.[9]

During these times, the idea that people had the right to defend their property gained widespread acceptance. Indeed, popular security devices of the times were wolf traps placed inside doors and windows to "snare" intruders and prevent break ins.[10]

Sir Robert Peel

In 1829 Sir Robert Peel, then Britain's Home Secretary, radically reformed the British police system. Through his "Peelian Reform" he organized all the different, and competing, police agencies into one unified metropolitan police force. Peel insisted that an effective and efficient police organization had to be non-military, professional, trained, and ethical.[11] Out of deference to Peel, London Police Officers are still referred to as "bobbies."

Peel is renowned for saying "The police are the public and the public are the police." According to Robert Gerden, author and private security consultant, in general, the police forces of Peel's time were more reactive than proactive. Private security would later fulfill the need for proactive security bent on crime prevention.[12]

EARLY PRIVATE SECURITY IN THE UNITED STATES

Unfortunately, the American colonists imported much of the crime and public disorder that existed in British society. They responded to the need to maintain order by establishing a night watch.[13] The first cities with night watches were Boston, in 1636; New York City, in 1658; and Philadelphia, in 1700.

During their patrol, members of the night watch would raise the "hue and cry" if they required assistance to deal with crime, public disorder, or an emergency situation. In many respects, they also served as an early fire department, as they were ever vigilant for any sign of smoke or fire. Left unchecked, a fire could easily destroy all the buildings in an early town or village.

As cities grew in size and the population became more diverse, the scope of crime forced public law enforcement and private security to move in separate directions. While policing became more reactive to events after a crime had been committed, private security focused more on preventing crime within specific areas.

Early Crime Prevention Tools

Cash Register

The invention of the cash register in the mid 19th century is a good example of the private security industry's preventive approach. As was true then, and now, internal theft by employees led to greater losses than external theft. The cash register was invented specifically to assist in controlling employee theft.[14]

Alarm Security Monitor

The first automatic burglary sensor was invented in 1853 by a Massachusetts inventor, Augustus Pope. His invention comprised electromagnetic contacts for doors and windows and was controlled by an on/off switch. In 1858, a Boston entrepreneur, Edwin Holmes, bought Pope's patent and established the first burglar alarm business. His clients were wealthy homeowners in Boston and New York City who leased the equipment.[15] His improvements to the alarm system included the following components:

Annunciator. Coloured tabs to show specific doors or windows that had been opened.

Clock. A timer to shunt the alarm in the morning to prevent false alarms by the movement of household staff.

Light. A switch to light up the affected area when an alarm was triggered.

Central Station. One location established to monitor a large number of alarms on a regular basis.

Galvanometer. An instrument to detect electric potential from an intruder.[16]

By 1872 Holmes had retained many business subscribers to his system and by the late 1870s, he had established his own force of Patrol Officers to respond to alarms. By 1880, the Holmes Protection Co. was monitoring every high-risk establishment in Boston, New York City, and Philadelphia.[17]

With the advent of telephones, alarm central stations could be notified by an alarm signal through telephone direct current circuits. ADT Security Systems Inc. held the monopoly on this process until the early 1970s.

Early Detectives and Security

The discovery of gold in California created a tremendous need for armed guards and Patrol Officers. As well, the movement of gold and money from the West Coast to the East Coast and vice versa created the need for protection of the cargo in transit. This need led to the rise of armoured express companies and private detective agencies to follow up on thefts and pursue the culprits.

Pinkerton National Detective Agency

Allan Pinkerton is credited with being the first person to establish a formal private detective agency. When he originally emigrated from his native Scotland, he had planned to settle in Canada but, at the last moment, went to Chicago instead. As a result of an investigation on Pinkerton's part, a major theft was prevented and, as his reward, Pinkerton was appointed as Chicago's first detective.

In 1850, Pinkerton resigned to form his own private detective agency. By 1853 the Pinkerton National Detective Agency employed five full-time investigators (four men, one woman). Pinkerton's specialty was protecting the railroads and thwarting any plots against them.[18] During the American Civil War, Pinkerton was appointed head of intelligence for the Union Army.

Pinkerton Law

In the summer of 1892, Carnegie Steel Company was negotiating with the Amalgamated Association of Iron & Steel Workers at their Homestead, Pennsylvania, plant. On July 1, 1892, the workers seized the plant. As the mayor of Homestead also belonged to the union, Carnegie Steel turned to Pinkerton to assist it in recovering control of the plant. Three hundred Pinkerton employees ended up in a pitched battle with 10,000 Carnegie Steel workers. Resulting gunfire left three Pinkerton employees and five steelworkers dead. The Pinkerton force surrendered and four days later the plant was liberated by state troopers.

An investigation by the U.S. Congress cleared Pinkerton and Carnegie Steel of any wrongdoing but indicated that "...the execution of laws should not be delegated to private individuals employed by companies."[19] In 1893 a law was passed barring the employment of Pinkerton and any other private detective agencies by the U.S. Government. This law is still in force and has become know as the Pinkerton Law.

Brink's

In 1859, Washington Perry Brink formed a truck and package delivery service in Chicago. He delivered the first payroll in 1891 through armoured car and courier service. Today, Brink's Inc. is the largest armoured truck service company in the world.[20]

William J. Burns Detective Agency

In 1909, a former U.S. Secret Service agent formed William J. Burns Detective Agency in Chicago. Until the FBI was established in 1924, the Pinkerton and Burns agencies were the only nationwide organizations providing national protection and investigating crimes across the country.[21]

The Rise of Private Security after World War II

After WW II there was a rapid expansion of private security's role. By the 1950s, private security had expanded to all areas of public and private life. During the 1960s private and public doubts were raised about the effectiveness of public police due to a combination of factors:

- The public and business sector's rising affluence and growing expectations meant they were prepared to pay for individualized service.
- Civil unrest and a significant rise in the national crime rate created a climate of unease.
- The political assassinations of the Kennedys and Martin Luther King, Jr. raised doubts about the effectiveness and efficiency of the police.

In response, the public, private business, and corporations turned to private security for protection. Vietnam veterans and young retirees from police agencies supplied a ready pool of qualified recruits.

Also during the time, the Bank Protection Act of 1968 was established to "promulgate rules and establish minimum standards with which each bank or savings and loan association must comply."[22] In addition, a litigious public and sympathetic judiciary began to hold property owners directly responsible for the standard of care and protection for those who ventured onto their property or place of business. Significant damage awards began to be won by victims who could demonstrate a lack of "reasonable care and protection" by the owners of the property where an incident occurred. The perception of safety became a factor that influenced people's choices in terms of where to shop, play, and go to school.

In 1975, the U.S. Department of Commerce reported that ordinary crime cost business over \$23 billion.[23] As well, over \$6 billion was spent on private security. In 1975 the National Advisory Committee on Criminal Justice Standards and Goals established a Task Force on Private Security to study and prepare standards and goals for private security persons.[24]

Terrorism

The rise of terrorism in the 1970s also created an immediate demand for greater protection by the public. People didn't care if this protection came from the police or from private security, as long as it was effective.

Standards

The rapid expansion of private security within individual companies and through contract guard services in the 1970s has given rise to a demand for standards. So too has the perception that a lack of training and supervision predominate the private security sector. We will explore standards and training further in Chapter 2.

Table 1.1 traces the debuts of private security firms within the United States.

Table 1.1	Early Private Security Firms in the United States	
Agency	**Date**	**Principal Activity**
Pinkerton National Detective Agency	1851	Protection of railroad assets
Wells Fargo & Company	1852	Transportation of goods
North West Police Agency	1855	Protection of railroad assets
Pinkerton Protection Patrol	1857	Provision of contract security
Holmes Protection, Inc.	1858	Central burglar alarms
Brink's Inc.	1858	Transportation of goods
William J. Burns Detective Agency	1909	Provision of contract security
Wackenhut Corporation	1954	Provision of contract security

Source: Gerden (1998: 19)

EARLY PRIVATE SECURITY IN CANADA

As in the United States, the establishment of national railroads provided much of the impetus for the development of private security in Canada. Private security in Canada came into being because there were no public police forces. There were no salaried Police Officers in Ontario until 1875 and as late as 1905, there were only six full-time Police Officers in Ontario.[25] In keeping with American tradition, the first Police Officer in Ontario was previously the head of detectives for the Canadian Southern Railway.

Many of the successful private security firms in the United States opened up branch offices in Canada. They had to quickly adapt to Canada's parliamentary political system and its legal system. Indeed, Canada was dominated by U.S. private security firms early on.

Early firms in Canada included Burns International Security Service (previously William J. Burns Detective Agency), Pinkerton Protection Patrol, Wackenhut Corporation, and Barnes. As well, many former Canadian Police Officers and military personnel established "homegrown" private security and investigation services in Canada including R.T. Brockbank & Associates, Controlled Risk, First Protection, and Ensign Security.

Provincial Licence Requirements

Private security (contract) companies are regulated in each province through provincial legislation. For the most part, in-house security personnel are not regulated. In Ontario, contract security guards are licensed as individuals under the Private Investigator's and Security Guards Act. As well, their companies must also be licensed under the same act. This act is administered and enforced by the Registrar, Private Investigators and Security Guards Section, Ministry of the Solicitor General. Ontario Provincial Police Officers who have been seconded to the Ministry of the Solicitor General assist in administration and enforcement through an Enforcement Unit.

Table 1.2 compares private security (contract) licence requirements in all Canadian provinces.

TABLE 1.2 Government-Regulated Positions Requiring Licencing											
Positions	YT	BC	Alta.	Sask.	Man.	Ont.	Que.	NB	NS	PEI	Nfld.
Private Investigators	X	X	X	X	X	X	X	X	X	X	X
Security Guards	X	X	X	X	X	X	X	X	X	X	X
Armoured-car Personnel	X	X	*					X	X	X	X
Locksmiths	X	X**						P			
Alarm Installer/ Response Personnel	X	X						P		X	
Security Consultants		X						P		X	
Canadian Corps of Commissionaires							X	P			
In-house Security		P								P	

Source: Gerden (1998: 37)

X = Licenced categories
P = Proposed licencing
*Only employers, not employees
** Regulated by another government department aside from the private security field

REVIEW QUESTIONS

Level A

1. (a) What was the Pinkerton Law?

   (b) Should it still be in force now and can you relate it to recent events in your province?
2. What are the advantages/disadvantages of a police agency being non-military?
3. Why is it important to study the history of private security? Discuss.

Level B

1. In a totalitarian state, there is no need for private security. Do you agree or disagree? Discuss and provide historical examples.
2. Should a police agency be run as a business?
3. What was the primary motivation behind the establishment of private detective and security agencies in the United States? Why was the government unable to fulfill this need?
4. Find out about each of the following professional associations regarding: contact number, Web site, certification programs, and publications. As well, speak to some of their members.
   - Association of Certified Fraud Examiners (ACFE)
   - Canadian General Standards Board (CGSB)
   - The Canadian Society for Industrial Security (CSIS)
   - The American Society for Industrial Security (ASIS)
   - The Federal Association of Security Officials (FASO)
   - The Canadian Alarm and Security Association (CANASA)
   - The International Foundation for Protection Officers (IFPO)
   - The American Society of Law Enforcement Trainers (ASLET)
   - The Ontario Association of Police Educators (OAPE)
   - National Association of Security Personnel (NASP)
   - The Commission on Accreditation for Law Enforcement Agencies (CALEA)

Level C

1. Dollar for dollar, who provides the more cost-effective and quality-conscious service: police or private security? Treat this as a business case study and expand on your answer to involve the burgeoning and popular "community policing" initiatives.
2. The railroads were responsible for the sustained development of the Canadian interior. How and why did the railroads contribute to the development of private security in Canada?

MODERN PRIVATE SECURITY

LEARNING OUTCOMES

At the conclusion of this chapter, you will be able to

- Provide a working definition of the term *private security*
- Distinguish between the roles of police and private security
- Identify the services provided by private security companies and state six core private security functions
- Distinguish between contract and in-house security providers

TOWARDS A DEFINITION OF PRIVATE SECURITY

One of the most frequently asked questions is "How many private security employees are there in Canada? In my province?" The answer to this question varies depending on who you ask and the specific province you're in. Some restrict private security only to licenced contract security staff while others would include in-house personnel. Are bouncers private security? What about a person whose role is 80 per cent reception duties and only 20 per cent security? What about a paid duty Police Officer working at a special event under the direction of a private enterprise? If those in the industry are confused about who should be counted as a private security employee, it is not surprising that our clients and members of the public are equally confused.

Does it really make a difference if there is no standard definition of private security? Until the scope, mandate, and definition of private security are agreed upon, we cannot begin the process of establishing training and performance standards for it. For that reason alone, a good working definition is important.

A working definition of private security must

- Incorporate both personnel and technological concepts
- Distinguish between public police and private security and those in between
- Include all areas of risk management; a somewhat utilitarian definition of risk being "anything that could hurt profit"

Table 2.1 offers a review of a number of definitions of private security and also indicates the shortcomings of each definition.

TABLE 2.1 Definitions of Private Security		
Definition	**Source**	**Comment**
Private security includes those individuals employed in a job whose principal component is a security function. They are privately employed, privately accountable, and have no special powers to maintain the peace. Peace Officer continuum: X————————X————————X Security CN police Police	Shearing et al. (1980)	Paid duty Police Officers are excluded.
Private security includes those self-employed individuals and privately funded business entities and organizations providing security-related services to specific clientele for a fee, for the individual or entity that retains or employees them, or for themselves, in order to protect their persons, private property, or interests from various hazards.	U.S. Private Security Task Force (1976)	Security who work for government institutions and the Canadian Corps of Commissionaires are excluded.
Private security can be defined as those individuals, organizations, and services, other than public law enforcement agencies, which are engaged primarily in the prevention of crime, loss, or harm to specific individuals, organizations, or facilities.	Gion Green (1981)	Those who manufacture, distribute, or install security products are excluded.
Private security is a profit-oriented industry that provides personnel, equipment, and/or procedures to prevent losses caused by human error, emergencies, disasters, or criminal actions.	Hess & Wroblesk (1992: 27)	Volunteer security is excluded.

Definition	Source	Comment
The security sector is an essential component in crime prevention, investigation, and protection of all people, assets and property. It involves all those who have an interest in, a concern for, and are beneficiaries of security. It is both a provider of security services and security goods (equipment). It includes all stakeholders: owners, employees, and organized labour; governments, corporations, and businesses; educators, standards organizations, and associations. It is both dedicated (in-house) and for hire (contract).	Second Conference of the Canadian Security Sector (1996)	This definition is the most inclusive.

Source: Compiled from data in Gerden (1998: 18–20)

THE ROLES OF POLICE AND PRIVATE SECURITY

Primary Function of Police

Notwithstanding the current focus on community policing—whereby police define themselves as a "service" and not a "force"—the primary function of the police has always been to apprehend criminals after crimes have been committed. This was true in Sir Robert Peel's day and, arguably, is still true today in this age of cutbacks and diminishing police resources.

Primary Function of Private Security

Traditionally, the primary function of private security has been to protect people, property, and information by preventing crimes from happening in the first place.

Police Concerns about Private Security

Some representatives of national and provincial police associations have been very critical of the private security industry and, although they do not provide specifics, claim that it suffers from lack of training, lack of supervision, and is "substandard and contrary to the public interest."[1] These critics have suggested that Security Officers "try to copy the police uniform to a degree…and it creates confusion in the public as to what the status of their authority is."[2] Critics have also said, "If you get some wannabe rent-a-cop out there, and one of them slaps somebody in the mouth, the public and the media are not going to say Joe…of (a security company) did such and such, they're going to paint law enforcement (with a) wide brush stroke."[3]

The fundamental concern of police is that in the eyes of the public, security is inextricably linked with them and that the image of police may be sullied by actions taken by Security Officers. This view arises partly from the fact that many security uniforms resemble police uniforms. Overall, such claims are questionable because they represent stereotyping in the extreme. It would be akin to stating that "all cops drink coffee and eat donuts." However, there are some elements of truth in these comments.

Some of the concerns raised by police have been addressed. In 1999 recommendations were made by the Private Security and Investigation Advisory Committee (PSIAC) to the Registrar, Ministry of the Solicitor General, Ontario, related to private security uniforming standards, baton use, and training.

The baton use recommendations have been implemented, as have the uniform standard recommendations. Security Guards are not allowed to wear a uniform or drive a vehicle on duty that may cause person(s) to believe they are Police Officers. However, issues related to training standards have not been resolved at the time of writing.

Private Security Population in Canada

There are inherent difficulties in establishing the number of private security personnel in Canada because

- The definition of private security varies across Canada
- Only certain sectors of private security are licensed
- There is a large part-time contingent
- The rate of security employee turnover is high (more than 100 percent annually for some companies)

Estimates for 1990–91 place Canadian private security personnel at 125,000 and public police at 55,000.[4] The ratio of security to police is 2 to 1. Gerden suggests that these numbers underestimate both police and private security numbers. He suggests that a more realistic ratio of security to police is 3 to 1.[5]

Today, the growth of the security industry is driven mainly by eight factors:

1. People's fear of crime
2. Cutbacks in public police resources and personnel
3. Privatization of many non-essential policing functions
4. Greater expertise of security personnel in the corporate sector
5. Globalization of the world economy
6. Growing number of security professionals who are certified through the American Society for Industrial Security (Certified Protection Professional [CPP]) or through the International Foundation for Protection Officers (Certified Protection Officer [CPO])
7. An increase in liability claims
8. New technologically complex crimes requiring a degree of specialization beyond the abilities of many police agencies

PUBLIC POLICE VERSUS PRIVATE POLICE

Some private security organizations have taken to calling themselves "private police." This type of direct reference to police is viewed negatively by some members of the policing community because they feel the public may construe such organizations as being associated with the police.

The term *private police* appears to have entered common usage and appears often in security literature. Some police representatives also object to the term *public police* to describe the police force. They assert "the police are the police" and the adjective "public" is unnecessary and may cause confusion in some people's minds.

Table 2.2 presents some of the more common titles associated with and services offered by private security.

TABLE 2.2	Security Titles and Services
Security Title	**Services**
Alarm Response Operative	The operative provides mobile response to alarms.
Central Station Operator	The operator monitors alarms and dispatches response units.
Close Protection Operative	The operative provides executive protection.
Loss Prevention Officer	The Officer provides plainclothes surveillance in retail stores to detect and apprehend shoplifters.
Patrol Officer	The Officer conducts mobile or static patrol of a predefined area.
Security Consultant	Anyone can call him- or herself a security consultant because there is limited legislation pertaining to this area. In general, it takes a minimum of 10 years of dedicated training and experience before someone has "expert knowledge" in any area.
Security Director	The director is the management representative at the site level.
Security Guard	The guard's role is defined by state or provincial legislation.
Security Officer	This term is now preferred to "Security Guard," but some provincial legislation still requires that "Security Guard" be displayed by contract security.
Technical Surveillance Operative	The operative sweeps for electronic "bugs" and other compromises.

Many of the positions described above are not entry level and may require a high degree of skill and specialized knowledge. The table does not include the variety of other positions that are unique to specific corporations.

There are a number of areas that were traditionally considered strictly policing functions that are now either being undertaken by, or being proposed to be undertaken by, private security. In Table 2.3, the lower the activity is in the list, the more directly it relates to a core police function.

TABLE 2.3	Private Security Functions
Activity	**Comment**
1 Issuing parking tags	This function has been ongoing for a number of years but was quite controversial when first introduced.
2 Alarm response	Private security actually responded to alarms before there were police departments.
3 Arrests	Private security has authority to arrest as does any private citizen. A Security Officer is not authorized to release those arrested. They must be turned over to a Peace Officer.
4 Fraud investigations	This function has been ongoing for a number of years.
5 Order maintenance	Mobile response to areas lacking Security Officer coverage.
6 Patrolling of public areas	This function has been ongoing for a number of years.
7 Transportation of prisoners	This area has been proposed to become a private security function.
8 Issuing of minor traffic violations	This area has been proposed to become a private security function.
9 Traffic control	This area has been proposed to become a private security function.
10 Release on promise to appear or on Provincial Offence Notice	This area has been proposed to become a private security function.

CONTRACT SECURITY VERSUS IN-HOUSE SECURITY

Contract Security

Contract security refers to security staff employed by a private security agency who provides security services to other organizations on a contractual basis.

In-house Security

In-house security refers to security staff employed directly by the company it provides security services for.

An ongoing debate has raged over the years as to the advantages and disadvantages of working for, or engaging the services of, contract or in-house security. Table 2.4 summarizes the advantages and disadvantages of each security type.

TABLE 2.4	Contract versus In-house Security: Advantages and Disadvantages	

Contract Security

Category	Advantage	Disadvantage
Turnover	Allows client to have unsuitable staff quickly replaced	High turnover rate
Training	Cost of training assumed by the security company	Often poor, inadequate training with no measurable standards
Remuneration	Tied to performance or in many cases, the hourly rate is site-specific	Often low pay with no benefits
Commitment	Larger commitment to the security company	May not have a strong enough commitment to the site from the client's perspective
Career path	Only limited by size of the security company	Entry-level security often thought of as a "dead end" job
Uniforming	Security company standard; better purchase price due to volume discounts	May not be exactly what the client needs
Liability	Limits the liability of the client company	Liability limitations determined by the degree of operational control exercised by the client

In-house Security

Category	Advantage	Disadvantage
Turnover	Low turnover	Expensive and difficult to get rid of unsuitable staff
Training	Site-specific skill training can be delivered "just in time"	Focus often very narrow
Remuneration	Increases tied to fixed budget	Additional costs re: benefits
Commitment	Focused on one specific site	No real place for a disgruntled employee to go
Career path	Possible opportunities within other departments	Limited opportunities in security role
Uniforming	One style of uniform	High price due to limited orders
Liability	Direct control over actions of employee	Unlimited liability

What the above tables indicate is there are no clear-cut answers to which type of security is best overall. Each company should consider all options and develop a clear business case before making a hiring decision. The overall trend has been an increase in contract security and a general decline in in-house security. The exception is large companies with 25 or more security staff that can readily support an in-house operation.

Security Guard or Security Officer?

The preferred title is "Security Officer" because it denotes a higher degree of professionalism. In Ontario, however, the Private Investigator's and Security Guards Act still requires that all persons acting in the capacity of a Security Guard must display the words *Security Guard* on their uniform.

Some might say, "What's in a name?" The word *Security Guard* conjures up extremely negative connotations. In the industry, some have suggested that a two-tiered designation be used to describe the position:

Security Guard. For employees with little or no training and no formal education

Security Officer. For employees with a high degree of training, post-secondary education, and professional designation and certification

LOSS PREVENTION AND RESOURCE PROTECTION DEPARTMENTS

Due to the increasing risk management role of security, many security departments have now been renamed "loss prevention" or "resource protection" departments. To be effective, such departments should also be capable of conducting investigations and crime analysis; completing security audits and reviews; and researching and making crime prevention suggestions.

By including risk management in its functions, private security can be viewed as a revenue-generating department rather than as just an expense. For example, how do you assign value to the Security Officer who investigates a burning smell, turns off a coffee pot, and saves the premises from burning down? Adopting new titles that reflect private security's expanded role may help raise the overall profile of the industry.

STANDARDS

There are no mandated national standards for private security in Canada. There has been a great deal of discussion regarding the requirement for standards in the private security industry. Specifically, those in the industry have strongly suggested that standards are required with respect to

- Recruitment and selection
- Training
- Supervision
- Uniforming
- Reporting

Clearly, standards cannot be used to determine if one product or service is superior to another. What they can ensure is that a base level of quality has been met. By adopting standards, private security companies provide reassurance to clients that a certain consistency will be applied with respect to the quality of product or services provided.

CALEA

For law enforcement agencies, the Commission on Accreditation for Law Enforcement Agencies (CALEA) has set quality standards for over 20 years. CALEA was formed in 1979 and now includes over 500 law enforcement agencies in North America registered to the CALEA Quality Standard. This includes eight police services in Canada: Brandon Police Service, Camrose Police Service, Edmonton Police Service, Lethbridge Police Service, Niagara Regional Police Service, Niagara Parks Police, Peel Regional Police Service, and Winnipeg Police Service.

With the recent changes to the Police Services Act in Ontario, and a stated intent from the Ministry of the Solicitor General to increase accountability and standardization of Ontario Police Services (e.g., institution of the Police Foundations Training Program), many more police services may consider registration to the CALEA Quality Standard. We are going to hear a lot more about CALEA in Ontario, and in Canada.

The major membership organizations that compose CALEA are:

- International Association of Chiefs of Police (IACP)
- National Organization of Black Law Enforcement Executives (NOBLE)
- National Sheriffs' Association (NSA)
- Police Executive Research Forum (PERF)

Contact information:
Commission on Accreditation for Law Enforcement Agencies Inc. (CALEA)
10306 Eaton Place, Suite 320
Fairfax, Virginia
220030-2201
U.S.
Toll Free: (800) 368-3757
Fax: (703) 591-2206
E-mail: calea@calea.org
Web site: **www.calea.org**

ISO 9000

An increasing number of private security companies are applying to achieve ISO status. ISO 9000 is a series of international standards establishing global requirements for quality management systems. The first standards were published in 1987.

ISO 9000 is unique in that it can be adopted by a broad range of companies and industries, including both the manufacturing of products and the provision of services.

An organization's quality management system, *not its products,* is registered to ISO 9000 Standards—specifically to either ISO 9001 or ISO 9002. ISO 9000 is a "guidance document" that tells you how to implement one of the other two Standards.

ISO 9000, or any quality system, provides for a management system to ensure that a company consistently documents what it says it does and then does what it says it has documented. Using a quality-system approach, the focus is on quality assurance not just quality control.

The ISO 9000 standards comprise 20 elements (19 for ISO 9002) that have been identified as being necessary for any business to consistently maintain a quality level expected by the customer. The standards provide the guidance and requirements for organizations looking to establish, implement, and maintain a quality management system.

Under ISO 9000, only the quality management system is certified, not the output of the system.

The following ISO references are available to supplement your knowledge:

Brumm, Eugenia K. 1995. *Managing Records For ISO 9000 Compliance.* Milwaukee, WI: ASQC Quality Press.

Clements, Richard Barrett. 1993. *Quality Manager's Complete Guide to ISO 9000.* New Jersey, NY: Prentice Hall.

Regel, Terry and J. P. Russell. 1996. *After the Quality Audit.* Milwaukee, WI: ASQC Quality Press.

One of the best ISO publications is *Quality Progress,* which is published monthly by the American Society for Quality (Tel.: 1-800-248-1946).

SECURITY TRAINING

In the past, lack of training has been a barrier to the recognition of security practitioners as true professionals. For a number of years, three organizations have provided professional certification programs:

1. **Canadian Society for Industrial Security**

   The Canadian Society for Industrial Security (CSIS) operates an Accredited Security Professional Program (ASP). Further information can be obtained through the CSIS Web site: **www.csis-scsi.org/educate.htm**.

2. **American Society for Industrial Security**

   The American Society for Industrial Security (ASIS) operates a Certified Protection Professional (CPP) Program that has been recognized worldwide as a benchmark in professional accreditation over the last 20 years. Minimum requirements for the CPP are nine years security experience with two years in a responsible charge position and the ability to pass the CPP qualifying exam. Further information can be obtained through the ASIS Web site: **www.asisonline.org**.

3. **International Foundation for Protection Officers**

   The International Foundation for Protection Officers (IFPO) offers a Certified Protection Officer (CPO) designation. Further information can be obtained through the IFPO Web site: **www.ifpo.com**

TYPES OF PREMISES PATROLLED BY PRIVATE SECURITY

The types of premises patrolled by private security can be broadly classified as follows:

1. Retail malls
2. Commercial office buildings (standard multi-tenanted office buildings)
3. Industrial buildings (factories, plants)
4. Institutional buildings (colleges, hospitals, universities, museums, art galleries, etc.)

5. Residential buldings (apartments, condominiums, from low- to high-threat sites)

6. Multi-use buildings (retail, commercial, and residential all in one complex)

7. Corporate head offices

8. Construction sites or other open areas (parks, etc.)

9. Special assignments (short-term assignments where security fulfills a basic protective service [alarm system out, fire alarm system down, etc.])

10. Government buildings (parliament buildings, provincial legislatures, etc.)

Each one of these complexes has its own challenges and security professionals must modify their patrol function to meet the needs of clients in each of the specific premises.

Basic Types of Security Patrols

The basic types of security patrols are:

1. Mall patrol

2. Special patrol

3. Lease-line violation patrol

4. Late opening/early closing patrol

5. Management delivery

6. Safety and fire hazards patrol

7. Parking area patrol

8. Perimeter patrol

9. Mechanical area patrol

10. Floor-by-floor or commercial office tower patrol

11. Stairwell patrol

12. Order maintenance patrol

13. Timed clock round patrol

14. Escort patrol (cash escort, personal safety escort)

We will examine these patrols in detail in the following chapters.

SELF-REGULATION OR GOVERNMENT REGULATION?

Currently within Ontario, contract security companies and Security Guards are administered and regulated through the Registrar, Private Investigator's and Security Guards Section, Ministry of the Solicitor General. The controlling regulation is the Private Investigator's and Security Guards Act. Recently, several security and investigation organizations suggested that the security industry be allowed to regulate itself using a model similar to those followed by other professions (i.e., doctors, lawyers, engineers, etc.).

Questions that arise are: Is the industry mature enough to accept the challenge? Can an appropriate business case be put together which would indicate a clear cost-benefit for proceeding with self-regulation? These are pressing questions that will be addressed over the next few years.

THE FUTURE

Without question, the private security industry is growing by leaps and bounds. There are definitely exciting career possibilities for those who are considering a career in this field. Clearly, the industry as a whole must adopt specific standards. Only then will private security personnel be perceived as true professionals. The industry has to "cycle out" of its low-bid mentality and take on a long-term perspective.

The concerns raised by some police association representatives (the merits of their concerns aside) must be addressed. There must be a true partnership and a spirit of co-operation between the law enforcement and private security communities. Co-operation and partnerships are occurring at individual levels, but the integration must be applied on a consistent basis. What we need to see is the type of partnerships between the policing community, the business community, and the college community that has been fostered by many progressive colleges and universities throughout Canada. There is some merit in the idea that the security industry should seriously consider integrating the CALEA and ISO 9000 models to develop one private security quality standard that can be applied across the country.

Progress Check

At this point the astute reader may be wondering why we have progressed two chapters into this textbook and have hardly even mentioned security patrols. What is going on? That is a valid question. We could have started our discussion by focusing on the "hard skills" of security patrols, but it is important to establish the fundamentals of the field before we address the details. Hopefully, you now know the basics that will allow you to fully appreciate the importance of the security patrol function.

REVIEW QUESTIONS

Level A

1. List five in-house and five contract security companies that you are familiar with. Rank them in the order that you would want to work for them.

    a. Group contract and in-house companies separately.

    b. Group both types of companies together.

    c. Choose three categories from Table 2.4 and compare the advantages and disadvantages of each company.

2. What are the advantages and disadvantages for a private security company in allowing its security employees to dress and act like Police Officers?

Level B

1. Why is it important to have a clear understanding of the term *private security* from the perspective of

   a. Government?

   b. The public?

   c. Private sector employer?

   d. The Security Officer?

Level C

1. Should private security companies be referred to as "private police"? Discuss.

2. What can be done on an individual and corporate level to reassure some members of the policing community who have expressed concerns about the poor training standards prevalent within the private security industry?

3

OFFICER
SAFETY

LEARNING OUTCOMES

At the conclusion of this chapter, you will be able to

- Explain the concept of total survival
- Distinguish between a Contact and Cover Officer
- Explain and apply the relative positioning concept
- Understand and apply the awareness spectrum

Note: You will not be able to articulate your application of force within the use of force model as this is outside the scope of this chapter.

TOTAL SURVIVAL: WHY IS OFFICER SAFETY IMPORTANT?

Security Officers are compensated for the time, effort, and dedication they apply to their profession. They are not being paid to "take the bullet" or place themselves knowingly into situations where it is very likely they will be killed or injured. Employers are obligated to supply Security Officers with the proper training, resources, and backup to meet all the challenges of the job. Security Officers are responsible for applying their training and consistently maintaining an "I will survive" attitude regardless of the circumstances.

Over the last 10 to 15 years there have been tremendous developments in officer safety and survival tactics. It is not enough just to read about these tactics, however. Security

Officers must apply them in a realistic, scenario-based environment. There are a number of professional trainers available who, for a modest fee, can provide Security Officers with practical training. If Security Officers cannot find a suitable training service, they may wish to contact the training department of their local police department. While training departments will not make specific trainer recommendations, they may be able to give you names of individuals who offer such training. As well, any of the security associations listed in the "Questions" section of chapter 1 can recommend qualified individuals who offer such courses. Security Officers must be very careful whom they choose to train them. Trainers may only be risking their reputations if what they teach is wrong—Security Officers are risking their lives.

Total Survival

It is not enough for Security Officers just to survive an encounter physically, they may also have to deal with the courts, their family, and their own internal selves. Ed Nowicki, survival specialist, describes *total survival* as "the physical, psychological, the emotional, and professional survival of an officer."[1]

Example

An armed suspect confronts an officer and, to survive, the officer applies lethal force resulting in the suspect's death.

The officer has achieved physical survival. However, he doesn't document his actions properly and cannot articulate the reasons for applying lethal force and, as a result, is charged. The company suspends him from active duty pending the outcome of the trial. This means his professional survival is in jeopardy. As a result of the stress of being charged, and the incident itself, the officer becomes very depressed (emotional and psychological survival) and his marriage breaks up. Even if the officer is ultimately acquitted, he becomes frustrated in his job and quits.

In this situation, the officer survived physically but did not survive psychologically, emotionally, professionally, or even financially. In later chapters, we will briefly review some of the areas Security Officers need to master to maintain total survival: documentation; patrol procedures; a positive attitude, etc. Throughout their training and education, Security Officers must become a "knowledge sponge," always looking for strategy and tactics that add to their ability to maintain total survival.

Nowicki summarizes the ideal approach to officer survival. "Officer survival is also an attitude; an attitude that requires a personal commitment to attain the skills and information necessary to meet the various challenges of law enforcement. This requires individual officers to reach beyond their limitations. It means never accepting defeat and looking at mistakes as learning experiences. If and when mistakes are made in critical situations, it means having the skills and attitude to survive the mistakes. The survival attitude is the winning attitude."[2]

PHYSICAL SURVIVAL ESSENTIALS

Contact and Cover Principle

On September 14, 1981, two San Diego Police Officers were killed by suspects who were originally stopped for misdemeanour offences. As a result, the roles of Contact and Cover Officers were developed to avoid a repeat of this tragedy.

A *Contact Officer* is a primary investigator. He or she initiates and conducts all the business of the contact and is responsible for the chain of custody of any evidence.

A *Cover Officer* protects the Contact Officer by establishing a "force presence." He or she devotes all attention to the action of the suspects and maintains a position of surveillance and control. He or she discourages escape attempts and prevents the destruction of evidence by assuming the best possible tactical position.[3]

Contact and Cover Officer roles must be used any time two or more Security Officers make contact with one or more unsecured subjects. These roles must be decided upon in advance of an encounter. However, officers must also understand that the roles can switch due to the nature of the encounter. In a two-officer situation, there must always be someone acting as Contact Officer and someone acting as Cover Officer. The ideal position for the Cover Officer is close enough to get a clear front and peripheral view of both the subject(s) and surrounding area.[4]

Police Officer fatalities were significantly reduced once the contact and cover principle was universally adopted. Although initially developed for Police Officers, it is even more appropriate for application by Security Officers given that most are not as well-equipped or as well-trained as Police Officers. For Security Officers who frequently work together, it is often useful for them to develop their own special codes that they can use when approaching contact and cover situations.

Relative Positioning Concept

The relative positioning concept is almost as important as the contact and cover principle. Relative positioning refers to the five positions around a subject that one can use when approaching a subject (see Figure 3.1).

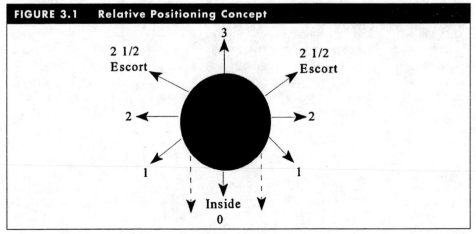

FIGURE 3.1   Relative Positioning Concept

The circle in the figure represents the subject. The dashed lines refer to possible movement of the subject. Each position is described below.

Position 0

- Inside position
- The area directly in front of a subject
- Most dangerous of all the positions
- Zero tactical advantage—should be avoided

Position 1

- Front and to the side
- Interview position
- Used for approaching subject

Position 2

- Directly to the side
- Used for approaching subject

Position 2 1/2

- Behind and to the side
- Escort position (when escorting a subject)
- Used when arresting subject

Position 3

- Directly behind the subject
- Used for approaching violent offenders

Note: Do not refer to this as the "ambush" position when articulating your actions; it does not go over well in court to suggest that you are "ambushing" the subject.

Although originally developed with the idea of approaching subjects, the same concept of relative positioning can be applied when approaching buildings or vehicles. The main entrance of the building would, of course, be the inside position.

Vehicle Threat Zones

On occasion, a Security Officer may be required to approach an occupied vehicle parked on the property that is being protected. These situations can be very dangerous, and any vehicle should be approached with extreme caution. The basic rule of thumb is: when in doubt, do not approach. Call for back up, or, if necessary, call for Police assistance. Basic officer safety can be heightened through awareness of vehicle threat zones encountered during an officer's approach to the vehicle (see Figure 3.2).

FIGURE 3.2   Vehicle Threat Zones

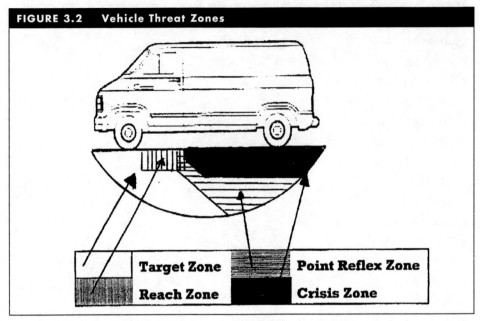

Source: Charles Remsberg, Calibre Press (1993: 280)

Crisis Zone

- A 20 in. (50 cm) wide strip (approximate width of a human body) running from the vehicle's rear bumper and ending about 10 in. (25 cm) away from the driver's window
- Also extends 10 in. (25 cm) from passenger window if passengers in back seat

Reach Zone

- Extends forward an arm's length from where the Crisis Zone ends.

Point Reflex Zone

- Also known as instinctive shooting—or "point and shoot"—zone
- Fans out from the back corner of driver's (or passenger's) window
- A 45-degree angle to the Crisis Zone

Target Zone

- Arcs from where it overlaps the Point Reflex Zone around to the front fender of the vehicle
- Security Officers should not approach or stand in the Point Reflex Zone or Target Zone because they can easily be shot with a firearm from someone in the front seat of the vehicle.

When approaching a vehicle, Security Officers should avoid the most vulnerable areas and approach through the Crisis Zone. This makes it more difficult for someone in the vehicle to take aim at them.[5]

It is, of course, understood that you would not approach a vehicle on the property you are protecting unless you feel comfortable in approaching it. If there are multiple occupants, or you cannot see into the vehicle, *do not approach the vehicle.* Monitor the vehicle and call for your backup or notify the police, if the situation warrants police attendance.

Awareness Spectrum

The awareness spectrum is a means of categorizing your level of alertness as you approach a potential crisis situation.[6] It is a tactical process that can be used to help Security Officers

- Operate at the proper level of awareness relative to the required degree of readiness that is needed for the given situation
- Detect early warning signs of a risk or threat
- Jump to a higher degree of alertness or readiness *in advance* of the situation escalating

Colours are used to indicate the various levels of awareness, anticipation, concentration, and self-control that frames the officer's mind-set.

Certainly, from a Security Officer perspective, an understanding of the awareness spectrum can compensate for a lack of handcuffs, batons, and firearms. Too often, Police Officers become complacent in their approach to a subject based on the faulty premise that their weapons will allow them to control whatever develops.

Colours of the Awareness Spectrum

Condition White. Environmental unawareness—this is the blissful state of most untrained security personnel.

Condition Yellow. Relaxed, but alert and cautious, and not tense. Constant 360-degree surveillance of people, places, things, and actions. This should be the continuous state of all on-duty Security Officers, especially when they are on patrol.

Condition Orange. A state of alarm.

Condition Red. What looks wrong, is wrong. The focus is now on the threat. The Security Officer acts to control it using whatever degree of force is required. All systems are go.

Condition Black. Blind panic.[7]

Unfortunately, all too often officers jump from Condition White immediately to Condition Black when a situation arises they did not anticipate, are not prepared for, and cannot deal with. When we are in a state of blind panic we can do some surprising things. There are documented cases of Police Officers who, while in a state of panic

- Pointed their finger, instead of their gun, at a suspect
- Threw their fully loaded gun at the suspect (these are true stories!)
- Removed their gun, duty belt, and handcuffs, placing them on a crowded sidewalk, and then approached the suspect

We will not be discussing the role that our central nervous system plays in our response, but the interested reader is encouraged to study Pressure Point Control Tactics (PPCT), where the role of the sympathetic and para-sympathetic nervous system is thoroughly addressed. Bruce Siddle, defensive tactics instructor, has assembled an impressive system of defensive tactics. Also, a number of instructors teach PPCT defensive tactics.

Contact information:
PPCT Management Systems, Inc.
500 South Ill. Suite 3
Millstadt, Illinois 62260
Tel.: (618) 476-3535

Also, we will not address the appropriate stances to adopt when interacting with a subject: open stance, ready stance, and defensive stance. These positions can only be adequately addressed in a defensive tactics course or use of force course where there is an opportunity for physical interaction.

Threat Assessment

Appropriate tactical thinking allows Security Officers to assess the risk in any situation they encounter and equips them to identify the appropriate response option. Figure 3.3 describes the threat assessment triangle. Three basic concepts are fundamental to successfully assessing any risk:

1. *Problem Area.* Any person, object, or site that may produce a hazard to the Security Officer.

2. *Area of Responsibility.* The exact location within a problem area from which an attack could come.

3. *Focus Point.* A clear and present threat that must be immediately controlled to protect oneself or someone else.[8]

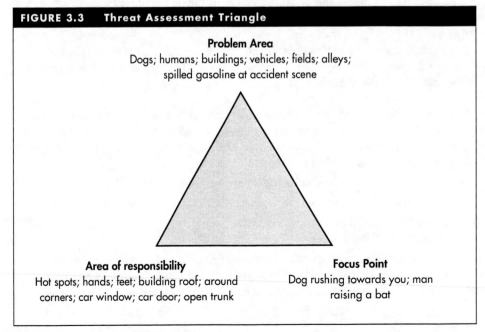

FIGURE 3.3   Threat Assessment Triangle

Problem Area
Dogs; humans; buildings; vehicles; fields; alleys;
spilled gasoline at accident scene

Area of responsibility
Hot spots; hands; feet; building roof; around
corners; car window; car door; open trunk

Focus Point
Dog rushing towards you; man
raising a bat

Source: Charles Remsberg, Calibre Press (1993: 55)

Once Security Officers assess risk and threat, they must

- Categorize the different elements of the scene they are approaching
- Establish priorities for control
- Formulate a tactical plan
- Monitor their safety as they progress through the occurrence
- Effectively neutralize any threats they encounter[9]

Frequently, both Security Officers and Police Officers are challenged by dogs during the execution of their duties. It is interesting that some would give a trained, black-belt martial artist only a 30 per cent chance of overcoming a trained Doberman empty-handed.[10]

A Security Officer's physical survival depends on the successful inter-relationship of a number of factors that establish his or her overall attitude: equipment, tactics, training, knowledge, fitness, and nutrition.

EMOTIONAL SURVIVAL ESSENTIALS

Security Officers are the first responders to a variety of emergency situations. No amount of training and experience can completely prepare them for the type of traumatic situations they may be called upon to react to, including

- Homicides
- Sudden deaths
- Fire, explosions, accidents
- The death of a child
- Serious woundings, etc.

In all likelihood, Security Officers will not "freeze"; their training will kick in and they will deal with the situation. This is the most likely scenario. However, emotional survival afterwards is critical. This is especially true if a Security Officer has been the victim of a violent encounter. At times, Security Officers may wish to seek counselling for Post-Traumatic Stress Disorder. Most organizations have a referral service where employees can seek assistance. Sometimes, the worst experiences come from co-workers who, to the best of their ability, try to help the affected Security Officer cope by making light of the situation. In many cases, professional counselling is a definite preferred option.

LEGAL SURVIVAL ESSENTIALS

By doing their job properly and by following their training, Security Officers should be ready, and willing, to take on any legal challenge that may arise from their actions. All too often, subjects lawfully arrested will bring assault charges against all Police and Security Officers involved. While, in most cases, these charges are unfounded, they still place a fairly high degree of stress on the charged Security Officer. One of the first things Security Officers should clarify with their employer is the depth of legal assistance the company is prepared to provide. Legal counsel is mandatory in situations where Security Officers have been charged or counter-charged. Security Officers must know where they stand with their organization on this point before the need arises.

Use of Force

Ultimately, a court of law is the final arbitrator that determines whether a Police Officer or Security Officer's use of force was justified. In Ontario, a use of force model has been developed which presents a force continuum (scale) that gives an officer the tools to articulate his or her reasons for applying a particular level of force. In brief, what follows is an outline of the current use of force model.

Level 1: Officer Presence. The officer's uniform establishes an initial display of authority.

Level 2: Tactical Communications. The officer uses his or her voice to persuade/influence the subject to comply with requests.

Level 3: Empty-handed Techniques. The officer applies soft techniques (pressure point control tactics) and/or hard techniques (strikes or blows).

Level 4: Intermediate Weapons. The officer uses a baton, pepper spray, etc.

Level 5: Lethal Force. The officer uses a firearm; strikes the subject's head with a baton; chokes the subject; hits the subject with a flashlight; hits the subject with a car.

Note: Disengagement is always an option at each level.

Certain impact factors (e.g., number of subjects, abilities comparison, demonstrated threat, situation, environment, time/distance) must be taken into account before a Security Officer decides on the appropriate use of force. As well, the profiled behaviour of the subject must be assessed (e.g., compliant, passive resistant, active resistant, assaultive, likely to cause death or serious bodily harm). Security Officers are called upon to articulate their application of force and explain the reasons for escalation. Table 3.1 establishes Security Officer, subject, and environmental impact parameters.

TABLE 3.1   Impact Parameters

Security Officer	Suspect	Environment
Age	Age	Time of day
Gender	Gender	Terrain
Fitness level	Fitness level	Available space
Health	Health	Number of subjects
Size relative to suspect	Size relative to Security Officer	Openness of the area
Skill level	Skill level	Weather conditions
Training	Martial arts training	Visibility
Prior knowledge of the suspect	Weapons	Weapons of opportunity

Many organizations adhere to the policy of Force +1. This means that Security Officers would be justified in using a level of force one level higher than what the subject is directing towards them. Unless Security Officers receive specific defensive tactics training and use of force training, it is recommended they restrict their response options to Level 1: Officer Presence and/or Level 2: Tactical Communications.

SECURITY OFFICER SAFETY CHECKLIST

Table 3.2 lists common sense security practices that should be followed by all Security Officers at all times.

TABLE 3.2 Security Officer Safety Checklist	
Strategy	**Rationale**
1 If you do not have any communication device (radio/cellular phone), you must call for and wait for backup prior to approaching a volatile situation.	You don't want to become part of the problem.
2 Test your radio before shift start and call in before entering and upon leaving radio dead zones.	Your radio is your lifeline.
3 Vary patrol routes and the start/finish times of your patrol.	You can reduce the ambush hazard by keeping the element of surprise in your favour.
4 Maintain a "safe" distance between yourself and any suspect. A minimum of 6 ft. (2 m) and more if weapons are suspected. Go to Condition Orange when subject closer than 21in. (53 cm) or the subject's arm's length (whichever is greater).	By maintaining the reactionary gap, you increase available tactical considerations. Officer safety = time + distance.
5 Identify specific areas of responsibility, problem areas, and focus points (i.e., suspect's hands, etc.).	You can make a quick threat assessment that allows for effective planning and implementation of your response.
6 Pause and evaluate any situation before entering it.	You can identify a safe "escape route" if needed (both for you and the subject).
7 Call for backup before entering any potentially volatile situations.	You can increase your response options.
8 Maintain Condition Yellow.	There should be no surprises.
9 If guns or knives are in evidence, leave the area and call for police.	Remember: think officer safety.
10 When making an arrest without a backup, the arrest should be made in visible areas (unless the suspect's friends are nearby).	Bystanders are more prepared to assist when only a single officer is present.
11 With multiple officers present, conduct arrests out of public view, if possible.	This approach avoids hostile crowd reactions.
12 Walk out from walls, especially when approaching corners or vestibules.	This approach reduces ambush hazard.
13 Do not enter premises by yourself if you suspect there has been a break and enter.	This approach is common sense.
14 Do not attempt to arrest multiple suspects alone.	This approach is common sense.
15 When approaching vehicles, the ratio should be two Security Officers to one vehicle.	Vehicles are potential ambush situations.

Table 3.3 lists basic personal safety tips that Security Officers should always consider when on or off duty.

TABLE 3.3 Basic Personal Safety Checklist	
Strategy	**Rationale**
1 Park your vehicle in a well lit, supervised area such as near a parking lot attendant's booth or near the elevator entrance.	You want to avoid making your vehicle a "target."
2 Alternate your parking spot.	Alternating routine helps avoid making your vehicle a target.
3 Don't leave anything in your vehicle that would identify it as belonging to a Security Officer.	This approach helps avoid making your vehicle a target.
4 Don't wear your uniform to work on public transit.	You can avoid being targeted.
5 Don't patronize liquor-licenced establishments at your site while off duty. At the very least, ensure you are with someone else.	Someone may seize the opportunity to attack you as a "pay back" for your earlier interactions with that person.
6 Do not release any personal information about your colleagues on site.	All personal information must be kept in the strictest confidence.
7 Don't wear articles of clothing or equipment that could identify you as a Security Officer when you are off duty.	You can avoid being targeted.

REVIEW QUESTIONS

Level A

1. (a) What level of force would you consider it to be if you used your Mag-Lite flashlight to strike an assaultive suspect?

    (b) What level of force would you consider it to be if you blocked someone's punch and then followed up with a knee strike to their leg?

2. Should you approach vans any differently than cars?

3. What would be your areas of responsibility in responding to a motorcycle accident in a parking lot? Describe some of the focus points.

Level B

1. Why is it important that you be able to articulate your reason(s) for using force?

2. How would you respond to a Security Officer who said: "I don't need to know anything about use of force, officer safety, or defensive tactics. All I ever do is sit at this access desk."?

3. Using examples, explain the contact and cover principle.

Level C

1. You have arrested a subject for assaulting a patron in a food court. (The subject provoked a fight with another patron and you witnessed the subject punch the patron.) When responding to the call, how would you conduct your threat assessment? Could you justify an arm-bar takedown of the subject, given that she was unco-operative and raised a fist as you approached? What environmental and impact parameters would you need to consider?

PATROL

PROCEDURES

LEARNING OUTCOMES

At the conclusion of this chapter, you will be able to

- Identify the main types of premises patrolled by private security
- Describe the nine core components of a security patrol
- Use a Subject Identification Form to identify suspect, vehicle, and weapons

TYPES OF PREMISES PATROLLED BY PRIVATE SECURITY

There are 10 basic types of premises where private Security Officers conduct security patrols. These premises can be broadly classified as follows:

1. Retail malls
2. Commercial office buildings (standard multi-tenanted office buildings)
3. Industrial buildings (factories, plants)
4. Institutional buildings (colleges, hospitals, universities, museums, art galleries, etc.)
5. Residential buildings (apartments, condominiums, from low-threat to high-threat sites)
6. Multi-use buildings (retail, commercial, and residential, all in one complex)
7. Corporate head offices

8. Construction sites or other open areas (parks, etc.)

9. Special assignments (short-term assignments where security fulfills a basic protective service [alarm system out, fire alarm system down, etc.])

10. Government buildings (parliament buildings, provincial legislatures, etc.)

CORE COMPONENTS OF PATROL PROCEDURES

Although the specifics of each premise will determine how security patrols are conducted, professional Security Officers must master nine core areas to safely and effectively conduct any type of patrol:

1. Officer safety

2. Observation

3. Deportment

4. Equipment

5. Site or account knowledge

6. Manner

7. Documentation

8. Public relations

9. Dealing with abnormal users and undesirables

1. Officer Safety

Attitude and common sense are the fundamental requirements necessary for Security Officers to consistently conduct their patrols in a safe and effective manner. Depending on the type of premise being patrolled, Security Officers may encounter various hazards including

- Violent individuals
- Persons with mental problems
- Criminals involved in criminal activity
- Environmental hazards (rough terrain, uneven ground, snow, ice, water)
- Mechanical hazards in machinery, fans, assembly lines
- Hazardous materials
- Animals
- Toxic waste

If Security Officers approach their patrols with the total survival attitude outlined in Chapter 3, they will minimize their chances of being injured or killed as a result of hazards encountered on the job.

2. Observation

The first guiding principle Security Officers must accept is: *there are no routine patrols.* Officers must conduct their 500th patrol with the same due diligence and observant behaviour as they did their first. An officer's powers of observation are what brings him or her back safely from patrol. All five senses—sight, hearing, smell, touch, taste—are essential.

Sight

Sense of sight is critical in an effective patrol. Our vision is not perfect, however, and is influenced by three parameters: distance from the observer, size of the object, and illumination that the object receives. For example, a Security Officer's colour rendering (the ability to distinguish different colours) is affected by the type of light illuminating an object or subject. He or she would not be able to recognize the familiar red serge of the RCMP uniform in low-pressure sodium lighting, as the jacket would look brown.

Things definitely look different under artificial light then they do under daylight. Be aware of such limitations. For example, someone you know well is easily recognizable to you in daylight, but you would only be able to recognize the same person at 1/10 the distance in full moonlight. The recognition parameters under moonlight are less than those available in full sunlight. As well, your positioning affects your perception of distance. A seated person will often overestimate the height of a standing person. This is something to keep in mind when recording witness descriptions.

People generally see what they expect to see and fill in any missing gaps. This can pose a problem if you are very familiar with your patrol route and overlook something that is out of place because you don't expect it to be there. You can sharpen your observation skills by randomly picking someone to observe as they pass by. Initially, pick out one or two prominent features and then double back on your patrol and see if you remembered that person's features. Your powers of observation will grow with practice and you will gradually be able to increase the number of features observed and the length of time you can remember them.

Pay close attention to the interior and exterior areas of any tenant areas that are within your patrol area. You should be able to recognize when something is out of place (i.e., blocked window area when the view is normally unobstructed) and can then take the appropriate action. You should also pay close attention to service people, contractors, etc. who normally frequent the area so you can recognize when someone tries to pose as them (this is a common ruse used by criminals). Be observant for routine habits of other staff regarding night deposits, etc. Rest assured, if you have identified the regular routine of a business person, it is possible that a criminal has as well. Pass your observations on to your supervisor for attention and follow up.

Scenario

It is 2:00 a.m. While on patrol, you notice a tractor trailer backed into the shipping area. The shipper/receiver is on the loading dock and two men you do not recognize are using a forklift to move items from out of the trailer onto the loading dock. Many of the items in the trailer seem to be strewn about haphazardly. The shipper/receiver has authority to be on-site, but this is the first time you have encountered such activity at 2:00 a.m. in your two years on-site. The shipper/receiver seems a bit nervous when you speak to him. Are you comfortable with this situation? What could be happening?

Faces Software

One of the most user-friendly means of obtaining subject descriptions is through the use of computer-based software packages such as "Faces." Faces allows for composite subject pictures to be developed using Windows-based software. Such pictures can then be digitally entered into a "security alert" based on the composite picture generated from witness description(s).

Contact information:

Interquest Inc.

Tel.: 1-888-824-3223

Web site: **www.facesinterquest.com**

The Subject Identification Form in Figure 4.1 identifies the features to look for when taking down descriptions of subjects. It should be considered as a sample only to be used for training purposes.

FIGURE 4.1   Subject Identification Form

SEX	AGE	HEIGHT	WEIGHT	RACE
Male ☐ Female ☐				White ☐ Non-White ☐

HAIR COLOUR
Black ☐   Blond ☐
Brown ☐   Brown ☐
Gray ☐   Red ☐
Silver ☐   White ☐

HAIR LENGTH
Bald ☐   Ear-Shoulder ☐
Above Ear ☐   Below Shoulder ☐
Ear Length ☐

HEADGEAR
(Colour/Type)

SHIRT/JACKET

TIE

PANTS/DRESS

FOOTWEAR
(Type/Colour/Laces)

SCARS/TATTOOS
(Specify type and location)

FACIAL HAIR

GLASSES

WEAPON   Yes ☐ No ☐
Handgun ☐
Knife ☐
Other ☐
Full Description:

VEHICLE Yes ☐ No ☐
COLOUR:_____
LIC#:_____
(Specify Prov/State)
MAKE/MODEL:_____
_____
NO. OCCUPANTS:_____
Direction of Travel:
_____

ACCOMPLICES: Yes ☐ No ☐

ARE THERE SEPARATE DESCRIPTIONS? Yes ☐ No ☐

YOUR NAME:		YOUR SIGNATURE:	
DATE COMPLETED:		DATE OF INCIDENT:	
CROSS REF. REP. #		POLICE OCC. #	

The form in Figure 4.1 should be used in conjunction with the Suspicious Person Form presented in Figure 5.2 in Chapter 5.

Hearing

Hearing is an important aid in identifying persons, places, and things. Security Officers should pay close attention to

- Activity noises such as breaking glass, knocking, bells ringing, etc.
- Voices (volume, pitch, accents)
- Motors—knowing what a "normal" motor sounds like so a different sound (e.g., high pitched whining) indicating an abnormal condition will be noticed
- Firearms (gunshots, ricochets, weapons being cocked, etc.)

Smell

Security Officers should also learn to distinguish between potentially dangerous odours including

- Gasoline
- Natural gas
- Gunpowder
- Coal oil and other petroleum products
- Other inflammables

Caution: certain substances and odours can temporarily block one's sense of smell, and increase the danger to an officer: chlorine gas, formaldehyde, acetylene, skunk odour, etc.

Touch

The sense of touch can be extremely useful for

- Examining doors and windows in the dark
- Checking tires, engines, or mufflers for warmth to determine if a car has been running recently
- Identifying certain types of cloth and paper
- Feeling the surface of stairwell doors for heat, which could indicate fire
- Checking a subject for weapons
- Feeling the pulse of a victim to determine if CPR is required

3. Deportment

A basic principle is: *if a Security Officer dresses and acts as a professional, he or she will be treated as such.* Security Officer deportment is critical on patrol and possibly when interacting with tenants, the client, and the public. A Security Officer's appearance has an immediate and lasting impact on those he or she meets. For these people, the Security

Officer represents the company. Thus, Security Officers should be comfortable with the image they project. Keep in mind, one never gets a second chance to create a first impression.

Uniform

Your uniform should be clean and neatly pressed. It must be your normal, regulation uniform. Any damage to your uniform should be reported to your supervisors and either repaired or replaced. Take pride in your uniform.

You

Your hair should be trimmed to company standard. For officer safety reasons, you should not wear excessive jewellery. You should be well-rested, showered, with fingernails trimmed. Take pride in your personal appearance.

4. Equipment

It goes without saying that Security Officers cannot effectively and efficiently do their job if they do not possess required equipment. Depending on company policy, regulation equipment can include

- Security licence
- Pen
- Notebook or memo book (the standard term is memo book)
- Timepiece
- Company policy manual (if required)
- Disposable safety gloves and carrier
- Radio
- Pager
- Flashlight
- Keys
- Pass card
- Soft body armour
- Handcuffs
- Side-handled baton
- Authorized firearm

5. Site or Account Knowledge

The more detailed knowledge Security Officers have of their site or account, the more effective they will be in an emergency and the safer they will be on patrol.

Doors

- Know which doors should be locked during the time of your patrol and which ones should be unlocked. Investigate any variations in the routine. Exercise caution when investigating as there could be a break-in taking place.
- Know which doors your keys provide access to. This is essential knowledge to have in an emergency. You don't want to be struggling with your keys when the fire department requests immediate access to an area.
- If you note signs of an obvious break-in, request assistance and *don't go in alone.*
- When you go through a locked door, lock it behind you. If you find it insecure on your return, you know somebody else was, or is, in the area.
- Look for the "shortcuts" throughout your site. This will allow you to "pop out" at locations where you would not normally be expected. Make the element of surprise work in your favour.

Briefing

You should be fully briefed at the start of your shift by the off-going officer you relieve, unless you are not relieving someone. That means you should arrive early enough to receive your briefing. If you show up one minute before the start of your shift and there is important information that the off-going Security Officer must pass on to you, then the person you are relieving will have to stay longer. This can lead to a buildup of resentment. Guess when *you* will be relieved?

6. Manner

Have you ever met somebody who just rubbed you the wrong way? You couldn't put your finger on it, but there was something about the person that instantly gave you reason to dislike him or her. Perhaps he or she was too abrupt, or too loud, or uncaring. Whatever the case, Security Officers do not want to be seen like that. If they don't already have it, they must develop a manner of approach and speech that is calming and projects an air of confidence without seeming to be cocky.

Proper breathing is important to maintain composure. Before going into a situation, take a couple of deep breaths and mentally compose yourself. Remember the first-aid course mantra: "Take five seconds to assess the situation." As well, in first-aid training, your objective is to prevent a condition from becoming any worse. You should have a calming effect on any situation you encounter. This composure and confidence will come with experience.

You can develop this air of composure in a couple of ways:

Join a public speaking club – For many, speaking in public is the ultimate horror. The confidence you acquire as a public speaker will transfer over to other aspects of your professional life.

Learn how to facilitate meetings and/or give seminars – Many clients welcome the opportunity for on-site security to give periodic seminars on a variety of topics to building or shopping centre clients.

There are some things you should not do.

- Don't be rude or abrupt.
- Never use sarcasm. It doesn't accomplish anything.
- Don't use humour inappropriately. If you do use humour, make sure you test for receptivity to ensure what you are saying/doing is appreciated by everyone.

7. Documentation

Nobody will ever know a Security Officer undertook a patrol if their actions are not documented. Normally, most private security organizations require that each Security Officer keep a personal notebook, or *memo book*, to document what they did on a shift-by-shift basis.

If you do keep a memo book, don't update your notes in a crowded area because that may shift you back into Condition White. Keep your memo book up-to-date so that in the event of an illness, accident, or emergency, your company can reconstruct the circumstances of the occurrence. When approaching a subject, *your memo book stays in your pocket*. If you have it out, it can only distract you from the business at hand.

Proper documentation will assist you in your desire for total survival; it will add to your credibility if you encounter a serious occurrence on your patrol. Your memo book and written reports are the first step in a documentation chain that establishes your credibility as a security professional and validates your actions. Poorly written, incomplete, or "rehearsed" reports or memo-book entries will shatter your credibility or, at the very least, make you appear less professional.

Your memo book is the most important documentation tool in your possession. Properly completed memo books can be used in court to refresh your memory regarding the circumstances you are presenting evidence about.

Thoughts have changed about the tense that should be used when making notes in your memo book or when completing a report. Previously, many in the police and security industries advocated the use of the third person because it was thought to make you appear more "professional" and "objective" in your description of events. Now both police and security personnel are advised to use the first person pronoun "I" when reporting their actions.[1] Part of the rationale is that writing in the first person is more natural and "unaffected." Using first person allows an officer to make a smoother presentation in court. This practice parallels the practice of having witness statements written in the first person.

Table 4.1 presents some basic guidelines to adhere to when completing your memo-book entries.

TABLE 4.1	Memo-Book Guidelines
Guideline	**Rationale**
1 Be consistent.	Consistency enhances your credibility. Start each shift entry by writing the same basic header (day, date, shift, post or location, road and weather conditions, equipment received, briefing notes, etc). Close each shift entry the same way for each shift (off duty, relieved by/no relief, your signature). Use the same ink colour throughout. Black ink is preferred for photocopying ease.
2 Be complete.	You can't rely on your memory to fill in the gaps one or two years down the road. "Tell me what the weather was like that day, officer?" How can you answer that question unless you wrote it down in your notes? "Well if you can't even remember the weather on that day, officer, how can you remember anything about my client?"
3 Be concise.	Your notes are not your diary. Only write down what is pertinent to your post or job function. Unnecessary information can be used against you if you are required to present evidence.
4 Be clear.	You must be able to read back from your own notes. There should not be any ambiguity or guesses on any material written down in your memo book. Print your notes in block letters. Although you will be slower at first, your speed will soon pick up.
5 Use simple words.	Few will be impressed by your imaginative vocabulary, least of all your client. Use words at the grade-8 level: "no" not "negative" "use" not "utilize" "went" not "disembarked" "spoke to" not "engaged in conversation with" "object" not "artifice" "saw" not "had occasion to observe" "left" not "exited" "told" not "advised" "later" not "subsequently"
6 Acknowledge your corrections.	Acknowledging changes enhances your credibility. Draw a single line through mistakes or changes. Make the correction. Place your initials above the correction.
7 Mark time of entry.	The time provides an unbroken, chronological record of all your shift activities.
8 Be accurate.	If necessary, draw a small sketch to describe a scene. Accuracy helps clarify events at the time of occurrence.
9 Follow review protocol.	Only allow authorized persons to review or have access to your memo book. Ensure your supervisor reviews and initials your memo book entries on a timely basis. Following protocol enhances personal and organizational professional credibility, and authenticates memo-book entries.
10 Retain your memo book for the established retention period.	The memo book is necessary for legal, financial, and knowledge-based review purposes. This guideline emphasizes the importance of documentation.
11 Write factual statements.	Only report what you observed through your senses. Your opinion should not appear in your memo book or in your reports.
12 Use the past tense of verbs.	You should be writing about what already has transpired.

Table 4.2 presents common memo-book errors.

TABLE 4.2 Common Memo-Book Errors	
What's Wrong	**How to Fix it**
1 Memo book is incomplete.	Take notes as soon as practical after the occurrence.
2 Memo book is inaccurate.	Use point form if necessary to adequately describe the occurrence.
3 Memo book is "refreshed."	Write your own notes before discussing the occurrence with others involved.
4 Memo book is unreadable and inaccurate.	Ensure that proper training and supervision occurs on a regular basis.
5 Memo book is missing or "lost."	Ensure that a proper system of documentation control is in place and adhered to.

8. Public Relations

Psychologists suggest that like behaviour attracts like behaviour. This means, if Security Officers go about their patrols displaying an open, friendly disposition, then that is probably what will be reflected back to them through encounters with tenants, the public, and their client. Security Officers should make a point of stressing to people what they *can do* rather than what they *cannot*.

While tact and diplomacy will not always work, it is important that you consistently display a warm, friendly, and efficient demeanour to the public. Look at yourself in the mirror and ask: What does a Security Officer look like and what does a Security Officer do? You should feel comfortable with standing up in a court of law and describing every one of your actions in detail.

When sterner measures are required, you must treat a suspect with a certain level of respect and dignity. Even if you are required to arrest someone, you have no reason to treat that person as less than a human being. There have been instances where suspects have refrained from killing Police Officers only because the officers had treated them with respect and dignity during the initial encounter.

9. Dealing with Abnormal Users and Undesirables

Part of a Security Officer's responsibility is to ensure that undesirables or abnormal users do not remain in the building to the detriment of its normal users. Remember, however, the decision to remove anyone must be based solely on the behaviour of the individual. A Security Officer cannot use appearance as a means of discrimination. Certainly, appearance is a visual cue that may attract attention initially (i.e., shoes tied with rubber bands, a person carrying several large garbage bags around, etc.).

Under no circumstances should you use abusive language or degrade an undesirable (even though he or she may be directing a string of profanity towards you), verbally or physically. Usually, the public takes the side of the underdog. If people see you, an able-bodied, uniformed Security Officer, mistreating an undesirable, you can rightfully expect that complaints will be lodged with the property management of the site.

Be firm when dealing with undesirables, but consider all options. For example, in many large urban centres there are organizations that provide immediate assistance (food, shelter/housing, health care, shower/laundry, clothing/blankets) to street people. Some organizations will even supply small business cards with their contact information on the card. Such cards can be carried by police and security and given to those who need assistance.

Find out the contact information for such organizations in your area. If you have to make an arrest, it may very well assist that person in receiving treatment. The fact that you carry and distribute these cards will act in your favour if you are required to attend court.

Don't let unnecessary roughness, abuse, or your use of public humiliation degrade your image, your company's image, or your client's image.

REVIEW QUESTIONS

Level A

1. (a) Name three items you should always have with you while on patrol.

   (b) Is it necessary to carry a flashlight during the day? Why or why not?

2. Do you agree an appropriate strategy for dealing with vagrants is to give them money? Will they always go away? Explain.

3. Name five things you would be looking for while patrolling

   - A boiler room

   - An underground garage

   - An apartment hallway

   - The food court of a busy mall at lunch time

Level B

1. How does the concept of total survival relate to the nine core components of patrol procedures?

2. Why is it useful to always keep your memo book up to date? Please provide at least three reasons.

3. How would you apply the contact/cover principle when you and your partner are approaching a male sleeping on the floor inside an Automatic Banking Machine area? Please take into account the restricted space limitations.

Level C

1. In the situation describe in Level B, question 3, you are the Cover Officer. The Contact Officer approaches the male sleeping on the floor and starts kicking him in the side. Because the subject is unresponsive, the Contact Officer continues kicking him until the subject cries out in pain, yelling that one of his ribs was broken. What actions would you take next? Be specific.

MALL PATROLS

LEARNING OUTCOMES

At the conclusion of this chapter, you will be able to

- Relate officer safety considerations to patrolling a mall
- Outline the specific functions of a mall Patrol Officer
- Explain the emergency response duties of a mall Patrol Officer
- Expand on some of the challenges associated with working as a mall Patrol Officer
- Comment on some concerns raised regarding private security's enforcement of the Trespass to Property Act

OFFICER SAFETY CONSIDERATIONS

Patrolling retail malls creates some unique officer safety challenges for Security Officers. Using the threat assessment model presented in Chapter 3, we will consider some of these challenges.

TABLE 5.1	Mall Patrol Threat Assessment	
Problem Areas	**Area of Responsibility**	**Focus Points**
1 Food court	Persons loitering	Hands Feet Weapons/objects seen Weapons/objects not seen
2 Theatre lineups in mall common area	Persons in line	Hands Feet Weapons/objects seen Weapons/objects not seen
3 Parking areas	Vehicles	Windows/Doors Open trunk
4 Washrooms	Persons loitering	Hands Feet Weapons/objects seen Weapons/objects not seen
5 Retail stores	Entrances/exits	Theft suspect running towards you
6 Mall roof	Roof edge	Thrown objects

Approaching Subjects

Security Officers on patrol in the common areas of a retail mall interact with numerous individuals. Most of these interactions will be positive in nature and will generally be requests for assistance and/or directions. At times, Security Officers will approach suspicious persons and engage them in conversation for a variety of reasons. The following five factors should be considered when approaching subjects in the mall:

1. Eyes
    - Watch where the subject's attention is focused. If he or she continues to focus on your baton, handcuffs or body armour this could be a potential pre-attack cue.
    - If the subject's gaze suddenly goes blank and he or she starts giving you the "thousand-yard stare," (i.e., looking right through you) this could signal an imminent attack.
    - If the subject briefly looks at an area of your body, he or she may be telegraphing where a strike will be focused.
    - Dilated pupils may indicate the subject is under the influence of a drug or narcotic, which may indicate potential unstable behaviour.

2. Hands
    - If a subject frequently "pats" an area of the body, this may indicate a concealed weapon.
    - Ideally, you want to be able to see the subject's hands at all times. If the subject starts to conceal either of his or her hands, this can indicate a pre-attack cue.
    - If a subject starts clasping and unclasping his or her hands, this may just be nervousness, but could also indicate an attempt by the subject to "psyche themselves up" into attacking you.

3. Feet
   • Watch the placement of a subject's feet. Is the subject in a natural "at ease" position or has he or she adopted a defensive or attack position?
   • What type of footwear is the subject wearing? Could weapons be concealed in a boot type of footwear? Certain gang members wear distinctive footwear.
4. Shoulders
   • Watch for the "shoulder shift" (a spontaneous shrugging of the shoulders) that can be a definite pre-attack cue.
5. Clothing
   • Pay very close attention to the clothing worn by the subject. Could it be used to conceal weapons? Is it non-seasonal (bulky, warm clothes in the summer), which may indicate a potential shoplifter. Look closely at any object carried by the subject.

PURPOSE OF A MALL PATROL

The purpose of a mall patrol can include one or more of the following:

Public Relations. You are the ambassador for the mall and often represent the first contact someone has when visiting an unfamiliar mall. Make sure you know the locations of most of the major retailers/services within your mall, or are carrying a map with that information available.

Theft Deterrent. Your presence may deter potential shoplifters/undesirables from stealing or creating a disturbance.

Lease-Line Violations. In many malls, mall management wants you to enforce merchant lease lines and caution merchants who extend their displays beyond their lease line without prior management authorization.

Late Opening/Early Closing Patrol. Most stores are contractually obliged to be open for business during posted mall hours. Frequently, mall management requires that you issue daily reports of all stores that open late or close early.

Suspicious Person/Activity. Specific areas may be prone to inappropriate behaviour or may attract a large number of abnormal users (e.g., washrooms, pay-phone areas, isolated alcoves) and will require additional checks. As well, you may have been provided with a suspect description from police or other sources and will be patrolling to see if the suspect is on-site.

Tenant Storefront Check. All tenant storefronts should be visually (if there is a sensitive door alarm) and/or physically checked after closing to ensure the premises are secure and there are no signs of break-in. You should make it a habit to check storefronts at the beginning and end of your shift if the stores are closed during that time. Make note of stores that are still active and pass this information on to your relief officer or return to check once stores become inactive.

Back-Corridor Patrol. The back corridors should be frequently patrolled to monitor for suspicious persons/activity and possible unauthorized move outs by merchants. Challenge any suspicious persons found in the back corridor areas. Ensure appropriate signage is in place to restrict access to back corridors.

Roof Patrol. Check the roof area of the mall for unauthorized persons, signs of attempted break-ins, and for items thrown up onto the roof (suspects will often throw weapons/stolen property/drugs up onto the roof if they spot police/security in the hopes they can retrieve it later). Check the roof area for possible mechanical failures, and fire and safety hazards.

Fire Equipment Inspections. Generally, all fire and life safety equipment (fire extinguishers, emergency lighting, exit lights, etc.) are checked by security on a regular basis and documented via a checklist. For added value, mall management may request these checks be extended to tenant areas.

FUNCTIONS OF A MALL PATROL OFFICER

Personal Interaction

Security Officers should be familiar with all of the mall merchants, but not overly familiar. If a Security Officer spends excessive time speaking to any particular person, others may question his or her intent and lodge a complaint. When walking by a store, a Security Officer should look into the store and catch the eye of the merchant to show his or her presence. Merchants will often nod, or smile, to acknowledge being seen. If something is wrong, or merchants see a potentially suspicious person, they are more prone to let Security Officers know if they have been in the habit of doing the above. This type of interaction only takes a moment, but it is a great public relations gesture.

When interacting with mall patrons, have pre-printed "mall conduct cards" (pre-approved by mall management) that can be issued to person(s) to clarify expected conduct within the mall. Figure 5.1 offers one example.

FIGURE 5.1　Mall Conduct Card

XYZ MALL

In consideration of other users of the smoking section food court, please respect the following guidelines:

1. Please use ashtrays provided.
2. Please place all garbage in the containers provided.
3. Due to the limited seating capacity, please use tables only when consuming food or beverages purchased in the food court.

Thank you for your patronage.

XYZ MALL MANAGEMENT

The contents of a mall conduct card can be modified to describe whatever behaviour there is a concern about.

Communication

It is vital for patrolling Security Officers to maintain some form of communication with someone who is in a position to contact emergency services or dispatch backup. In larger malls, there may be a base station radio room, or a designated information centre may also provide this central communication function. If Security Officers are on patrol by themselves without any direct means of communication, they must be particularly careful in approaching subjects.

All communication equipment used by the Security Officer should be tested at the start of each shift. As well, the Security Officer should advise when he or she will be entering radio "dead zones" and advise once he or she has left that area.

Specialized Functions

At times, patrolling Security Officers may be asked by supervisors or mall management to perform specialized functions over and above their regular duties:

Management Deliveries to All Stores. This function is an excellent public relations opportunity for you to get to know each merchant.

Lockouts. You may be asked to accompany a bailiff and/or locksmith on a store lockout.

Vehicle Count. You may be asked to record the total number of vehicles in the parking lot or garage (used for marketing purposes).

Cash Escorts. You may be asked to escort mall merchants to the bank or night deposit area. There are certain things you should/should not do when conducting cash escorts:

- Do not carry the cash.
- Where possible, stagger the times of deposits.
- Go directly to the night deposit. Don't stop to conduct other business along the way.
- Don't resist if a robbery attempt is made. Your priority is to protect your life and safety and that of the merchant you are escorting and the public.
- If you observe suspicious persons frequenting the night deposit area, escort the merchant back to his or her store and then attend with other security and/or Police Officers to speak to the suspicious persons.
- Walk two or three paces behind the person you are escorting on the side they are carrying the money.

You may find these activities boring and unrelated to security, but they are obviously important or mall management would not be prepared to pay your company to have you do them.

Emergency Equipment

You must know the nature, and function, of all emergency equipment in your mall. Typical emergency equipment includes

- Fire extinguishers
- Emergency oxygen supply
- Emergency gas shut-off valves
- Sprinkler valve shut-off

Suspicious Persons/Activities

What constitutes a suspicious person or suspicious activity? The nature of what makes a person or an activity suspicious can vary with the time of day and nature of the establishment. Persons loitering outside a jewellery store could be engaged in a pre-theft surveillance and would be considered suspicious. The same persons loitering outside an arcade may be a nuisance but would not necessarily be considered suspicious. If Security Officers are in doubt as to the reason why someone is in the mall, nothing prevents them from establishing contact and asking the person if they can help.

Example

You notice a middle-aged male standing near the pay telephones by a children's play area. He is not talking on the telephone and appears to be looking at a number of different children. What follows is a possible course of action on your part.

Security: Good day, Sir. How are you today?

Subject: I'm okay thanks.

Security: I noticed that you have been waiting here for awhile. Is there something I can help you with?

Subject: That's okay.

Security: Are you waiting for somebody?

Subject: Why would you want to know?

Security: For the sake of the children in this area, we monitor this area closely and we will speak to anyone we see remaining in this area, if they are not with a child.

Subject: Oh.....I see. Yes, I am waiting for my child. She is the young girl in the red jacket. (He waves to the child, and she smiles and waves back.)

Security: Thank you, sir.

Subject: Thank you.

This conversation could have gone differently, depending on the responses of the subject. Had he been belligerent or not able to establish a reason for his presence, the Security Officer could have backed off, continued to monitor the subject and called for a second officer to attend as a Cover Officer. A subsequent follow-up conversation with the subject could possibly end with security directing the subject to leave the area or leave the mall. Make absolutely sure, of course, that the subject does not have children there.

Never ignore situations like the above, or accept what people say right away without further probing and/or validation. Of course, you would document the above encounter as a suspicious person. Even though it turned out okay, you did not know that at the time. If the subject decided to complain about you talking to him, your supervisor and/or mall management would already have a copy of the report and would be in a better position to respond to the complaint.

Description of Suspicious Persons

A number of categories are useful when describing suspicious persons. Table 5.2 provides a detailed list.

Table 5.2	Describing Suspicious Persons
Category	**Description**
Race[1]	White Non-white Unknown
Complexion	Light Medium Dark
Speech[2]	Arabic (ARA) Chinese (CHI) Croatian (CRO) English (ENG) Filipino (FIL) French (FRE) German (GER) Greek (GRE) Gujarati (GUJ) Hungarian (HUN) Italian (ITA) Jamaican (JAM) Korean (KOR) Persian (PER) Polish (POL) Portuguese (POR) Punjabi (PUN) Spanish (SPA) Tamil (TAM)
Build	Medium Slim Heavy Muscular
Eye Colour[3]	Black (BLK) Blue (BLU) Brown (BRN) Green (GRN) Gray (GRY) Hazel (HAZ) Maroon (MRN)
Hair Colour	Black (BLK)

Blond (BLO)
Brown (BRN)
Grey (GRY)
Red (RED)
Silver (SIL)
White (WHI)

Hair Length	Bald
	Ear-shoulder
	Above ear
	Below shoulder
	Ear length
Hair Style	Afro/curly
	Dyed
	Straight
	Wavy
	Brush/box/cut
	Shaved
	Toupee
Deformities[4]	Amputation
	Birthmark
	Mole
	Scar
	Tattoo
	Other
Medical Condition	Not applicable (N/A)
	Physically challenged (specify)
	Intoxicated
	Emotional disability (specify)

---

[1] Be very sensitive when recording race descriptions. For example, don't ask a subject, "What is your race?" Mark down what you observe. The usage of race as a descriptor has been criticized as being potentially racist. We are not identifying racial origin, however, but are using a generic descriptor to help in identification purposes.
[2] No one expects Security Officers to be linguistic experts, but they should have some idea of the various languages used by persons who frequent their mall.
[3] The designation BRN-BLU would be used to denote a brown left eye and a blue right eye.
[4] The description of the deformity should be added to the text.

Suppose you are completing your sixth suspicious person report of the day at a site with a site code of 700305 on Saturday, October 7, 2000, at 11:15 p.m. Your report number would be

Report Number: 700305-00-281-2315-6

Site Code	Year	Day of Year (From 1 to 365/366)	Time of Incident (0001 to 2400)	Suspect Number (for that day)
700305	00	281	2315	6

This report number then becomes a unique identifier for that suspect and can be used in an electronic tracking system.

See Figure 5.2 for a simple version of a Suspicious Person Form that includes all of the above information.

FIGURE 5.2 **Suspicious Person Form**

SUSPICIOUS PERSONS		
DATE	**REPORT NUMBER**	
TIME	**SECURITY OFFICER**	
	EMPLOYEE NUMBER	

SITE ADDRESS

SPECIFIC LOCATION

SEX:	**AGE:**	**COMPLEXION:**	**RACE:**
HT:	**WT:**	**BUILD:**	**EYES:**

MARKS:		**DEFORMITIES:**
LOCATION:		**LOCATION:**
HAIR COLOUR:		**FACIAL HAIR:**
HAIR STYLE:		**SCARS/TATTOOS:**
SPEECH:		**LOCATION:**
CLOTHING:		**MEDICAL CONDITION:**
HEADGEAR:		**SHIRT/JACKET:**
FOOTWEAR:		**PANTS/DRESS:**
POSSESSIONS:		**WEAPON:**
JEWELLERY:		

VEHICLE: Yes ☐   No ☐   Possible ☐

COLOUR	**LIC#**	
MAKE/MODEL	**NO. OCCUPANTS**	

ASSOCIATES:

COMMENTS: (attach on separate sheet if necessary)

YOUR NAME	**YOUR SIGNATURE**	
DATE OF REPORT	**CROSS REF. REP. #**	

Storefront and Corridor Checks

All tenant storefronts should be visually (if there is a sensitive door alarm) and/or physically checked after closing to ensure the premises are secure and there are no signs of break-in. You should make it a habit to check storefronts at the beginning and end of your shift if the stores are closed during that time. Make note of stores that are still active and pass this information on to your relief officer or return to check once the stores become inactive.

The back corridors should be frequently patrolled to monitor for suspicious persons/activity and possible unauthorized move outs by merchants. Challenge any suspicious persons found in the back corridor areas. Ensure appropriate signage is in place to restrict access to back corridors.

Insecure Stores

If you find a store insecure when it should normally be secure, the following steps should be taken:

1. Check the area for signs of forced entry. If forced entry is evident or you have reason to believe an unauthorized person is in the store, *do not go into the store without other security and/or backup. Monitor the exterior of the store and wait for backup to arrive.*

2. If forced entry is not evident, notify the key holder and, if requested, accompany the key holder into the store. It is not a good idea to enter the store prior to the arrival of the key holder. If you are able to, remain outside the store and monitor the area until the arrival of the key holder. Your site policy will clarify what is expected of you.

3. Complete a full report documenting all your actions and the result (i.e., store secured or left insecure at the request of the tenant).

Safety Hazards

Security Officers should always check the areas they patrol for actual and potential safety hazards (e.g., fluid/liquid spills, tripping hazards, young children climbing/playing in areas where they could be injured). It is not enough for Security Officers to merely report such hazards; they must do everything they can, for liability reasons, to ensure the public does not remain exposed to the hazards.

Example

You find an ice cream spill on the mall floor and notify maintenance. Unless a higher priority occurrence develops, you should remain by the spill (or cone it off) until the mall cleaners can attend to it. If you just walk away and somebody slips on it before it is cleaned up, then the mall owners, your company, and you personally can be held liable for damages.

One moment's worth of prevention can be worth hundreds of thousands of dollars. You should also record in your memo book all safety hazards encountered and actions taken. Depending on your site, records of the above may be kept. Such reporting can be of great assistance in establishing due diligence for any potential liability claim.

During the winter months, security is often tasked with monitoring mall parking lots and mall sidewalks for ice and snow buildup. Depending on the policy established, Security

Officers may be required to notify mall maintenance or a snow removal contracting service to attend to the buildup. In particularly severe cases, Security Officers should also have access to snow/salt supplies to take proactive steps to ensure mall entrances are passable. The spreading of salt and sand should not be a primary security function, however.

It is often useful to maintain a formal weather and surface condition log. In addition, you should always be noting road and weather conditions in your memo book at the beginning and end of each shift. You should also note when the weather changes. Such documentation will prove invaluable if an occurrence arises where weather may be a factor.

Responding to Emergencies

What is an emergency? A good operating definition of an emergency is any condition that requires immediate action and if left unchecked would cause injury or death to any person or damage to property. That is a fairly broad definition but it does cover most of the situations security may be called upon to deal with in a mall.

Typical emergencies patrolling Security Officers encounter or respond to include

- General accidents (e.g., slip and falls)
- Assaults
- Bomb threats
- Elevator entrapment
- Fatalities
- Fights or other major disturbances
- Fires
- Floods
- Gas leaks
- Lost children (Why do we consider this an emergency?)
- Medical emergencies (e.g., heart attack, choking—especially in restaurants or the food court)
- Power failure
- Robberies or attempted robberies
- Sexual offences
- Vehicular accidents

Your site orders should indicate specific actions you are to take in the event of any emergency situation. In addition, it is expected that you are trained and certified in first aid and are competent to deal with medical emergencies. If you are not trained in first aid, you should seriously consider obtaining such certification.

When advised of an emergency situation, you should follow these steps:

1. Obtain exact details of the emergency from the person reporting it: What is the nature of the emergency? Is anyone injured? Have weapons been seen? Are the involved parties still on-site? What is the exact location of the emergency? Have emergency services been advised? Ensure emergency services are notified.

2. Determine if there are other Security Officers available to attend with you.

3. Make sure you have your disposable plastic gloves with you.

4. Proceed directly to the area of the emergency at a brisk pace. Generally, try to avoid running in public areas, but use your discretion—if you were laying on the ground with a suspect kicking your head, then you want your backup to get there ASAP.

5. Monitor the crowds and mall conditions while en route to the emergency situation. If there are suspects, they may be going past you.

6. On arrival at the emergency, assess the situation and prioritize your response.

7. Clearly establish who the involved parties are (i.e., victim, witness, suspect, etc.).

   Example

   You respond to a motorcycle/automobile accident in the mall parking lot and see a number of people milling about.

   Q. Is anyone injured? (If it is not clear who the injured party is).

   Q. Who was the driver of the blue car?

   Q. Who was the operator of the motorcycle? (Don't assume that because someone has a motorcycle helmet on that they are the operator.)

   Q. Who was a passenger in the blue car/motorcycle?

   Q. Who witnessed the accident?

8. If you can delegate others to assist in some capacity, do so. It builds confidence on the part of those around the area (you look and act like you know what you are doing).

9. Deal with the emergency in accordance with your training and company/site policy.

10. When other Security Officers arrive, quickly brief them on the situation and what you have done.

11. When emergency service personnel arrive, note their time of arrival, unit numbers, badge numbers, etc. Quickly brief emergency personnel on the situation and what you have done. If persons are to be transported to a hospital, confirm with the ambulance driver what hospital they will be taken to. If possible, obtain the ambulance run number. (There may not be time for this, but if there is, ask for the run number.)

12. Complete and file a full report and ensure both management and your company contacts have been advised.

Crowd Control

A *crowd* is group of individuals assembled together for a common, lawful purpose. A *mob* is a group of like-minded individuals assembled for an unlawful purpose.

When provoked, a peaceful crowd can quickly turn into a mob. The sight of a member of a crowd being arrested can precipitate the onset of a mob. Security Officers will often be called upon to assist in crowd control (e.g., theatre lineups, special celebrity events, special grand openings). When event planners know in advance there will be a large crowd assembled, planning and preparation must take place to ensure there are sufficient staff (i.e., police, security, management, maintenance, cleaning staff) and resources (e.g., stanchions, barricades, directional signs, bullhorns, radios, etc.) to deal with the event. As well, all staff must be fully briefed and aware of their functions.

Crowds are easier to control if they are provided with a clearly designated area to assemble and if instructions are clearly and frequently repeated to them. As well, crowds want to see the rules consistently enforced. For example, if there is a lineup, the line will not tolerate "line jumpers" and large-scale disturbances may result if Security Officers do not enforce the rules. As the crowd forms, it is useful for security and police staff to be present and interact with the crowd members. This makes controlling them later an easier task because the crowd members are in a good mood. If arrests have to be made, make sure they are done outside the view of the crowd. Above all, do not try to be overly authoritative in dealing with crowds. They are doing what officers ask on consent. If there are 15 000 of them and 20 Security Officers, security is not in much of a position to force the issue.

We will not address how to deal with mobs, riots, or demonstrations as that is beyond the scope of this textbook. Specific training courses exist that address these issues. Most major cities have public order units in their police departments that are specifically tasked to deal with such matters.

Lost Children

For parents, losing a child while out of the home can be one of the most traumatic experiences they will endure. Unfortunately, many busy shopping centres average about two or three lost children per day. Sometimes more.

Each site *must* have a specific, written procedure that indicates how security should react when dealing with lost/found children. (If there is no procedure, speak to your supervisor. There should be one.) What follows is a generic approach based on commonly accepted best practices for dealing with lost/found children. It is meant to supplement your site's existing policy.

Why should a lost child procedure be in place?

- A procedure ensures all staff know what to do so they can start searching immediately.
- Time is critical. Even a three-year-old can cover a large distance in a short period of time.
- Delay in starting the search can be fatal.
- Proper procedure helps positively identify whomever a found child is turned over to. You don't want to turn over a found child to anyone other than the parent or guardian legally responsible for the child.
- Using a procedure may reduce potential liability.

Why are there lost children?

- Inattentive parent(s) (how often have we heard the refrain "I only took my eyes off him/her for a second!")
- Busy, congested shopping areas (especially around holidays)
- Kidnapping (for ransom or for sexual assault)

Which sites experience lost children?

Any site where there are people with children can have lost children. Statistically, retail malls, special events, museums, special attractions, and amusement parks are more likely to have lost children. At certain special events (e.g., Royal Agricultural Winter Fair) specific areas are designated for lost children to go to (they are made attractive to the child) and individuals (in addition to security staff) are hired to help lost children.

Dealing with Parents

Do not expect parents to be calm and reasonable when they are reporting their child is lost. In many cases, they are angry with themselves for losing the child (or angry with the child for becoming lost) and very afraid that something terrible will happen to the child if the child is not immediately found. These conflicting emotions can often be redirected as hostility to the attending Security Officer (i.e., whatever he or she is doing isn't enough). Be aware of this possibility and stress to the parents you need certain critical information (name of child, description, clothing, age, area last seen, and the name, address and phone number of the parents) to assist in the search. Update parents frequently on what is being done. Keep parents with you or out in the common area where they can be contacted. You don't want the parents running around the mall once you have located the child—you want to know where the parents are.

What To Do When a Child Is Reported as Lost

The following steps should be taken when a child is reported as lost:

1. Have a pre-arranged signal to alert all staff (security, cleaners, maintenance, etc.) of a lost child (e.g., Code 10). *Do not* broadcast over the PA or radio "We have a lost little girl."
2. Whoever may be in a position to receive a lost child report should be aware of specific critical questions to ask the parents: name of parents and child, age and physical description of child, gender, and last known location.
3. Security should attend to and speak with the parents to confirm the above information.
4. *Everyone* (security, cleaners, maintenance) should take part in the search. In general, a lost child should take precedence over any other occurrence other than an immediate, life-threatening one.
5. Large anchor stores in the mall (Sears, Wal-Mart, Loblaws, etc.) should be immediately advised and should conduct their own search within their areas.

Areas to Search

1. Washrooms (Men's and Women's)

   • If you notice a child in one of the cubicles with an adult, wait in the washroom area until they exit and you can confirm it is not the lost child or, if you feel that the child is being attacked and in need of immediate assistance, call for backup and enter the cubicle. Be sure you can articulate your reasons why.

   Note: Child abductors have been known to carry a set of child's clothing with them. They force the child they have abducted to change clothing to confuse searchers (e.g., you are looking for a small girl in a blue snow suit and might not pay attention to one in a red snow suit being carried by an adult).

2. Food Courts

3. Parking Areas

   • Unattended three-year-olds have been found wandering around busy mall parking lots.

4. Pet Stores

5. Merchant Areas

   • Ask each store to thoroughly check within its area. Young children are experts at hide-and-seek. They think it is a game.

6. Toy Stores

   • These stores are a child magnet.

7. Any store with visual displays may attract young children.

Notifying Police

If a child under 10 years of age has not been found within 15 to 20 minutes of being lost, you should notify the local police and broaden the area of the search. Again, update the parents or guardians of the search status.

Locating Children

When the lost child has been located:

   • Verify with the child that it is his or her parents or guardian they are being turned over to

   • Obtain positive identification from the person you turn the child over to

   • Write a full report (very important for statistical and liability purposes)

Found Children

An event somewhat less stressful (for you) is when a lost child has been found. On those occasions, you should follow these steps:

1. Go to the area where the child is.

2. Stay with the child. Obtain as much information from the child as possible (their name, age, etc.—most importantly, the name of their parents/guardians who brought them to the mall).

3. If the names of the parents or guardians are known, broadcast their names over the PA and request they come to a specific location. *Do not* broadcast there has been a found child.

4. When talking to young children, move down to their level or raise them up to your level (e.g., have them sit on a counter). If the child "clams up," try to find someone in the mall who has experience dealing with young children and ask them to come to your location to talk to the child.

5. Avoid, if possible, taking a young child back to the security office with you.

6. If the parents have not been located within 30 minutes, notify your local police. They will attend to and take possession of the child. Make sure you obtain the name and badge number of the Police Officer who takes the child. As well, obtain a contact number from the Police Officer for the parents to call in case they show up after the officer leaves.

7. When releasing a found child to anyone, obtain positive identification from whoever will be receiving the child. Verify with the child they should be with that person.

8. If the child seems afraid to go with the person *or* you are unable to confirm identification of the person and are suspicious about their legitimacy in receiving the child, *do not* release the child. Advise the person you have to notify the police. This is something to be very firm about. If the parents argue, let them talk to the police dispatcher over the phone.

9. Complete and file a full report.

As a proactive measure, mall management could institute a lost child program in the mall involving all tenants, mall management, and security. Selected stores might display a distinctive logo that identifies them as a "safe location" for lost children, or a place parents can go for assistance in reporting a lost child. This type of program is good public relations for the mall and can also include the local police.

Protecting Children

Unattended Children

In a Vehicle. If you encounter young children left unattended in a vehicle, monitor the vehicle and have the owner of the vehicle paged. On hot or cold days, when the life or safety of the child may be in jeopardy, immediately remove the child from the vehicle via the safest means possible and notify police.

In Common Areas. Treat the unattended child as you would a found child.

Suspicious Persons

Pay particular attention to persons who may frequent washrooms or areas where young children play. Challenge anyone who you deem suspicious. They are in your area by invitation and can be directed to leave should the circumstances warrant it. Again, be very sure you can articulate your reasons, and file a complete report.

Enforcing the Trespass to Property Act

In Ontario, the Trespass to Property Act provides regulations that allow property owners, or agents of the owners, to regulate the activity on, or in relation to, their private property. Section 2 of the act outlines three offences:

1. Entering on to premises where entry has been prohibited

2. Engaging in an activity that has been prohibited

3. Failure to leave the premises immediately upon being directed to do so by the occupier or a person authorized by the occupier[2]

Enforcement of the act can be through the owner, or an agent of the owner. Providing that letter of agent status has been granted to security, Security Officers protecting the property of the owner can enforce the act on behalf of the owner. They can arrest any person on the property who commits any of the above offences.

Used properly, the Trespass to Property Act is an extremely effective tool that allows private security to maintain a safe environment for all users of the property. It is crucial, however, that security enforce the act in relation to a person's behaviour. The act itself does not require this. For example, a Security Officer can arbitrarily direct someone to leave the property and that person is obliged to do so or risk arrest by the Security Officer and possibly incur fines, if convicted. The offence, in this case, is committed as soon as the person fails to leave. Practical considerations dictate that security base enforcement on the behaviour of individuals.

Anyone arrested by security under the act must be immediately turned over to a Police Officer. Clear guidelines must be established by the mall and the Security Officer's company as to how the act is to be enforced. In particular, there should be some consistency as to how long people should be barred from the mall. The duration of the bar should be in relation to the severity of the person's behaviour. For example, minor disturbance might warrant a one-month bar, theft might warrant a one-year bar, and assaults against security or weapons offences might warrant a longer bar. In general, it is not prudent to bar someone from the property indefinitely as the courts will often react negatively to such a practice unless there are very extenuating circumstances.

Security Officers should properly document all occurrences relating to their enforcement of the act. As well, separate files should be maintained on those who have been barred. There should also be a review process in place where, for example, if a person wishes to contest their bar, or they would like to be allowed back on the property, mall management or the security supervisor/director should be prepared to meet with the person and review the situation.

If security abuses its authority to apply the Trespass to Property Act, it can, and has, been challenged through the Charter of Rights, Freedom of Association Provision, and can also face civil consequences. In 1987, a task force under the then Chairman of the Ontario Human Rights Commission Raj Anand reviewed the application of the Trespass to Property Act in Ontario on publicly used properties as it related to discrimination against youth and minorities. One of the recommendations of the task force was that owners of publicly used properties (e.g., shopping malls) be severely restricted in their application of the act. Many businesses and security groups made submissions opposing these proposed changes. They were not enacted, but the task force report makes for interesting reading because it suggests what can happen if security abuses its authority.

For further reading, see the following:

Anand, Raj. 1987. *Task Force on the Law Concerning Trespass to Publicly Used Property as it Affects Youth and Minorities.* Toronto, ON: Ministry of Government Services, Publication Services.

Missing Persons

Occasionally, you may be advised by police of missing persons. In many cases they may be juveniles or elderly persons who wander from their home or a seniors' residence. You should have some means of filing this information, posting it in your work area for all other security staff to see, and notifying other tenants/employees on-site. In the case of missing persons, you can greatly assist the police by co-operating in the search.

Found Persons

At times, you may find someone in the mall who appears disoriented; the person may be elderly, have mental problems, or suffer from a condition such as Alzheimer's disease. On those occasions, you should follow these steps:

1. Ask the person if you can help him or her.
2. Ask for the person's name, address, and phone number.
3. Ask the person if he or she is on any medication. Look to see if the person is wearing any type of Medic Alert bracelet.
4. If the person requires immediate medical attention, call for an ambulance and render first aid (if you are qualified).
5. If the person gives a phone number, call the number and see if there is a caregiver at that number who can attend your location.
6. If the person cannot provide any information, notify police. If possible, try to obtain a photo of the person, with consent, for future reference.
7. Complete and file a full report.

Proactive Suggestions

Know the demographics of your area. If there are several seniors' residences nearby, contact them to introduce yourself and obtain contact information in case you need to notify them. Let caregivers know you are there to assist. They may let you know in advance if someone in their care is prone to wander.

Juveniles

Runaways

The problem of juvenile runaways is chronic in many large urban areas, especially in the summer months. Malls are a prime area these young people head to. Again, know the demographics of your area. Be aware of the schools in your area and when their break times are.

If you see young, school-age persons on your property during school hours, not accompanied by an adult, and you know they are not on a break, approach them. Ask them why they are there. Your job will be easier if you have established preliminary contact with principals, vice-principals, guidance teachers, and school attendance officers in your area. They may even start calling you to see if any of their students are at your location.

Be creative. With your company and client's permission, offer to conduct a seminar at schools in the area to present what the expected conduct is while students are on mall property. A project that has proved very successful in the past is to invite local students and their teachers to the mall itself. Students can produce a video for class that has interviews with mall management, security, and some mall merchants.

Gangs versus Groups

One thing that must be clearly established is exactly what constitutes a gang. Often, mall patrons complain about all the "gangs" in the area. What they are really talking about are the "groups."

A *gang* is a group of individuals joined together with a common criminal intent. A *group* is a collection of like-minded individuals joined together with a common purpose.

It is vital for security to be able to distinguish between the two. In many cases, people automatically associate any type of graffiti with "gang activity," when in fact it may be *taggers* or "juveniles" who mark their initials or attempt to duplicate common gang symbols. Taggers may be a nuisance, and they do destroy property, but they are not generally thought of as "gangs."

True gang activity is identified by

- True gang monikers (markings)
- Gang-style dress and/or evidence of hand symbols being used
- Significant fights between groups as opposed to fights between individuals
- Significant sightings/findings of gang-related weapons (guns/knives)
- Information from the local police that suggest there is gang activity in the area

You should attempt to establish links with your local youth bureau; it can be invaluable in identifying known gang members who may frequent your area. When dealing with bona fide gang members, exercise extreme caution. Your best weapon is intelligence (i.e., know the names, addresses, and street names of all the local gang members). If you are confronted by a group of gang members you know as individuals, its members will be less inclined to engage in criminal acts when they realize you know who they are as individuals. It takes a concerted effort on your part to gather this information, but it can be done and has proven to be very effective in deterring criminal acts.

If possible, photograph any graffiti and arrange with mall management for it to be removed immediately. If gang activity is rampant in your area, you may wish to arrange with police to hold an area stakeholders' meeting to address the problem. Again, this approach has proven to be very successful in deterring criminal acts.

REVIEW QUESTIONS

Level A

1. Distinguish between "groups" and "gangs." Give examples.
2. Identify five things you should be looking out for while patrolling a mall.
3. State three offences outlined in the Trespass to Property Act of Ontario.

Level B

1. State five common groups you would expect to encounter within a retail mall environment. Why are they groups and not gangs?
2. While conducting a cash escort, the person you are escorting says he just wants to go into a coffee shop for a minute to buy a coffee because this is the only time he has to do so. What would you say and do?
3. What strategies might you suggest to mall management to prevent students from loitering in the mall smoking area after school?

Level C

1. As the director of security at the mall, you have been invited by the principal of a nearby high school to come in and give a presentation to students. Prepare a memo for your mall manager indicating why you should/should not attend. There have been repeated problems involving youths from the high school loitering in the mall during lunch hour and after school.
2. You have arrested a suspect without incident and are waiting in the security office for police to attend. The police dispatcher advises you that things are very busy and it will be over half an hour before a car can respond. It is 5:00 p.m., the time your supervisor goes off duty. He tells you he has to go and cannot stay. Although you don't have officer safety concerns regarding the suspect (she has been checked for weapons and is handcuffed), you are concerned about the length of time nobody will be patrolling the mall. What would you say to your supervisor and what further actions could you take?
3. You are the security director at a complex that is frequented by juveniles. A 13-year-old girl approaches you and asks if she can talk to you privately. You go back to the security office (leaving the door to the office open and blinds drawn back). She starts crying and says that one of her "friends" raped her at a party the other night. You ask her if she needs medical assistance and if she is willing to talk to a Police Officer. She says, "No. He told me his friends would kill my brother if I talk to the police." You know of her "friend" from previous encounters and had previously arrested him for trespass offences. He is currently barred from your complex and you have his complete information on file. You also have a fairly good working relationship with the area youth bureau. What would you do? Be specific.

PARKING
PATROL

LEARNING OUTCOMES

At the conclusion of this chapter, you will be able to

- Relate officer safety considerations to patrolling a parking garage
- Outline the specific functions of a garage patrol
- Describe a patrol route you would follow during a typical garage patrol
- Identify specific areas within the garage to check for abnormal users

OFFICER SAFETY CONSIDERATIONS

Patrolling parking garages creates some unique officer safety challenges for Security Officers. Using the threat assessment model developed in Chapter 3, we will consider some of those challenges.

TABLE 6.1	Parking Patrol Threat Assessment	
Problem Areas	**Area of Responsibility**	**Focus Points**
1 Parking areas	Vehicles	Windows/Doors Open trunk
2 Line of parked cars	Person(s) crouched down behind the cars	Hands Feet Weapons/objects seen Weapons/objects not seen
3 Stairwells	Persons loitering	Hands Feet Weapons/objects seen Weapons/objects not seen
4 Garage floor	Near parking areas	Oil spills Gas spills
5 Cement pillar	Person hiding	Hands Feet Weapons/objects seen Weapons/objects not seen

A parking garage attracts a variety of undesirables: thieves attempting to break into vehicles, vagrants loitering in the garage stairwell areas, and muggers waiting to ambush garage users. Lighting is generally poorer in the garage and there are numerous potential ambush hazards (line of parked vehicles, pillars, stairwell doors, etc.). When patrolling the garage, Security Officers must be on the lookout for two very real threats: careless drivers whose vehicles may strike them and undesirables who may attack them.

Use Your Senses

When you first enter the garage, pause for five to ten seconds and tune in to your surroundings.

Look for signs of movement—you may have startled someone trying to break into a car.

Listen for sounds of breaking glass, slammed car doors, footsteps, closing stairwell doors, voices, persons laughing.

Smell the air—be on the alert for any gas smells.

Be on the alert for carbon monoxide fumes. Check to see if the garage ventilating fans are on. They should be on if the garage is fairly active. If you find yourself feeling dizzy and nauseous, *exit the garage immediately and get some fresh air*. Notify the fire department and do not allow anyone into the garage until after the fire department has measured carbon-monoxide levels and given the "all clear." Remember: Carbon monoxide is a colourless, odourless gas. You will quickly be overcome by it if you don't get fresh air immediately.

If someone is breaking into a vehicle, he or she will usually have a tool of some sort—generally, a screwdriver. Therefore, *assume anyone breaking into a vehicle is armed.*

Maintain Communication

There are many dead-zone areas within parking garages where your radio will not transmit or receive. You should be aware of where those areas are and exercise the appropriate level of caution while in those areas. In an emergency situation, if you have no other means of communication, consider pulling one of the fire pull stations. That will bring assistance to you and potentially scare off anyone who may have been challenging you.

APPROACHING OCCUPIED VEHICLES

Be aware of the vehicle threat zones (see Figure 3.2 in Chapter 3) and avoid remaining in the Target Zone. Be particularly cautious of vans (you don't know how many people are inside them) and vehicles with tinted windows.

Listed below are some strategic considerations that have proven to be helpful in conducting safe and thorough garage patrols:

- Always have a flashlight with you when patrolling a garage. It is useful for checking vehicle interiors and lighting up dark areas underneath vehicles. If there is a power failure, you don't want to be lost in the garage without any light source.
- If there is any doubt in your mind as to your safety, don't approach the vehicle alone. Wait for backup or contact the police for assistance.
- Always write down the licence number of a vehicle in your memo book before you approach the vehicle.
- Challenge anyone you find working on a vehicle in the garage. Unless they have arranged for prior approval, they have right of access to the garage only to park their vehicle and to exit or access their vehicle. They are not entitled to remain inside their vehicles (sleeping or otherwise) for lengthy periods of time or to do maintenance work on their vehicle. You should check with your supervisor or the management of the property to verify what they consider acceptable behaviour by individuals in the garage.
- Always work out your escape route when approaching vehicles in the garage. For example, if the driver accelerates towards you or brandishes a weapon, do you know in advance what your escape route will be?

DEALING WITH UNDESIRABLES AND VAGRANTS

The temperature inside garages is generally warmer than the temperature outside. During the winter months, street persons may frequent unused or isolated areas within garages. Be particularly vigilant when checking garage stairwells. Look for signs of recent occupancy: urine on the floor, empty bottles, garbage bags, etc. From an officer safety standpoint, it is generally safer to walk "up" the stairwells as anyone you encounter can flee "up" the stairs. (i.e., start at the lowest level within the garage and walk up the stairwells to the ground level.). Note: the opposite direction is recommended for Stairwell Patrols in commercial buildings (see Chapter 10).

When speaking to undesirables (abnormal users) and vagrants, keep in mind the points discussed in Chapter 4 on how to deal with such people. In an isolated, underground garage you should be in Condition Orange when approaching a suspicious person. Assistance (even at a large account with backup officers) can take three to five minutes or longer.

Consider the following points when approaching suspicious persons in the garage:

- If you have a radio, call in your exact location (garage level, pillar number, spot number) and state that you are approaching a suspicious person. Indicate a time frame when you will be radioing back to advise on status.

- Use your flashlight as a distracter. If the person has been in the dark, your bright light will momentarily startle them and give you some additional time to conduct a threat assessment.

- Do not approach the person in a manner that "pens them in." Let them have an escape route. Even if they run away, you have done your job.

- Remember: Disengagement is always an option.

- Check your surroundings carefully to make sure there are no other persons in the area or hiding in the stairwell.

Be direct and assertive in your movements. Don't give the impression you are sluggish, tired, or afraid.

GUIDELINES FOR ESCORTING INDIVIDUALS TO VEHICLES

Frequently, you will be asked to escort individuals to their vehicles that are parked in the garage. Walk the person directly to the vehicle and shine your flashlight inside the vehicle to make sure there is nobody inside. Wait a few minutes nearby until the person starts the vehicle and pulls out of the parking spot. This ensures the vehicle is operable and the person is able to leave. You don't want to walk away and then find out later they were attacked because their vehicle had been disabled and they could not leave.

Often, garages will have a parking attendant during specific times. It is a good idea to introduce yourself to the attendant and check on his or her well-being while you are doing your garage patrols. That individual may also come to your assistance, so it is important to establish a good working relationship.

ABANDONED/STOLEN VEHICLES

Depending on the size and usage patterns of the garage, it is a good idea to record the licence numbers and locations of all vehicles parked in the garage after hours. Frequently, stolen vehicles are left in garages and on surface lots. If you suspect a vehicle is stolen, notify the police, who will verify its status. Depending on the relationship you have with the police, some police dispatchers will run a quick check for you over the telephone to verify if a vehicle is stolen. Others will not advise you of the status and will insist on dispatching a Police Officer. This is understandable, for if they don't know you, you could have stolen a car yourself and were just using a pretext call to determine if the car had been reported stolen yet! You can avoid this concern by always providing a direct call-back number and letting the police know in advance what your site telephone number is. Again, it is very important that you develop a good working relationship with the police.

If you have access to the Internet, you can verify whether a vehicle is stolen through the Canadian Police Information Centre (CPIC) Web site at: **www.nps.ca**. This Web site can also be used to verify if licence plates and other property have been reported stolen.

If a vehicle is abandoned but not stolen, management may wish to consider having the vehicle towed, because allowing it to remain in the garage (in possibly decrepit condition) sends the wrong signal to normal users of the garage.

Fully document any occurrence involving vehicles in the garage. This would also include the licence numbers and descriptions of vehicles being operated in a dangerous manner.

REVIEW QUESTIONS

Level A

1. What obvious officer safety concerns would you have when patrolling a parking garage?
2. From an officer safety perspective, if you are patrolling the garage stairwells, why is it safer to start from the lowest level and walk up to ground level?

Level B

1. When patrolling an underground garage, how can you use the convex mirrors to your tactical advantage?
2. Why is it a good idea to check on the condition of any fire extinguishers in the garage periodically (particularly on Victoria Day weekend)?
3. Why is it a good idea to write down the licence number of a vehicle in your memo book before you approach the vehicle?

Level C

1. If you have access to the Internet, use a search engine to find out crime prevention information related to parking garages. (Hint: Use the word CPTED or Crime Prevention Through Environmental Design and parking garages as keywords.)

PERIMETER PATROL

LEARNING OUTCOMES

At the conclusion of this chapter, you will be able to

- Relate officer safety considerations to conducting a perimeter patrol
- Outline the specific functions of a perimeter patrol
- Describe a patrol route you would follow during a typical perimeter patrol

OFFICER SAFETY CONSIDERATIONS

While conducting perimeter patrols, you should constantly scan your immediate vicinity and the area around you for tripping hazards, moving vehicles, suspects, and any other potential threats.

TABLE 7.1	**Perimeter Patrol Threat Assessment**	
Problem Areas	**Area of Responsibility**	**Focus Points**
1 Parking areas	Vehicles	Windows Doors Open trunk
2 Buildings	Building corners	Hands Feet Weapons/objects seen Weapons/objects not seen
3 Roof	Roof edge	Thrown objects

What are you looking for?

While conducting perimeter patrols you should be looking for any, or all, of the following:

Suspicious Vehicles.

Suspicious Persons/Suspicious Activities.

Insecure Perimeter Doors. Follow appropriate officer safety procedures when checking the interior of insecure perimeter areas (see Chapter 5)

Signs of Forced Entry. Do not enter without backup

Safety and Fire Hazards. Examples include wooden pallets, cardboard left outside the receiving area, and the strong smell of gas near the gas-metre area

Burnt Out Lights.

Damaged Perimeter Fencing.

Use your senses. Especially your sense of hearing, as sound will travel far at night. Listen for the sound of voices, laughing, slamming perimeter/car doors, breaking glass, and gunfire. Before starting your patrol, briefly close your eyes and wait one to two minutes to allow your night vision to become operable.

Be alert for any animals on the loose. In particular, stray dogs will often frequent the premises at night looking for scraps of food.

PATROL ROUTE

Plan your route in advance to ensure all critical areas are covered. Don't fall into the routine of always following the same route. If possible, pop out periodically from your building to do mini-perimeter spot checks. As well, periodically pop back into the building and then return to your perimeter patrol. Keep the element of surprise working for you.

When patrolling, it is useful to adopt the *outside-in* strategy. For example, start at the outermost perimeter location and work your way in. If a breach is found in the outer perimeter, there is a high likelihood the suspects will be somewhere within the inner perimeter.

If you are carrying a radio, periodically advise the person monitoring your transmission as to your location and status. Be aware of any radio dead zones on the perimeter and advise your backup before you enter them and after you have left them.

APPROACHING OCCUPIED PARKED VEHICLES

Approach parked vehicles on the perimeter in the same manner you would approach them in an underground parking garage patrol (see Chapter 6). Check on the well-being of any person(s) found in the vehicle. In particular, be very alert for vehicles running with their headlights off. A suspect could be conducting a pre-attack survey. Mark down the licence number of all vehicles you find parked during your perimeter patrol. During the winter months, occupied vehicles left running can result in carbon monoxide poisoning to vehicle occupants, should the exhaust system be faulty.

EQUIPMENT NEEDED

The following equipment is normally required to conduct safe and efficient perimeter patrols:

A Flashlight. Test the flashlight before starting the perimeter patrol to make sure it is working.

Appropriate Outerwear. Whatever the season and weather conditions, make sure you are adequately protected from the elements.

Keys to Allow You Back Inside the Building. It can be very embarrassing to lock yourself out of the building you are supposed to be protecting. It frequently happens, though.

A Watch or Timepiece

Proper Shoes/Overboots for the Terrain and Weather Conditions

Gloves. They will protect your hands if you have to handle any objects during your perimeter tour.

REVIEW QUESTIONS

Level A

1. Why is it appropriate to use the "outside-in" strategy when conducting perimeter patrols?
2. During the winter months, what additional safety hazards should you consider?
3. If your site is a low-rise building, why is it a good idea to monitor the roof area when conducting a perimeter patrol?

Level B

1. While conducting a perimeter patrol, you hear the screech of tires and notice two vehicles completing "donuts" in your parking lot. There are no other vehicles in the parking lot at this time. What would you do? Comment on any specific officer safety considerations.

Level C

1. How would you respond to one of your colleagues who boasts she can complete a perimeter patrol in under 10 minutes? (It has always taken you almost one-half hour to complete the same perimeter patrol.)

MECHANICAL ROOM PATROL

LEARNING OUTCOMES

At the conclusion of this chapter, you will be able to

- Relate officer safety considerations to conducting a mechanical room patrol
- Outline the specific functions of a mechanical room patrol
- Describe the abnormal conditions to look for while on mechanical room patrol

OFFICER SAFETY CONSIDERATIONS

The principal hazards encountered by security during mechanical patrols include:

- Tripping hazards (e.g., loose cable, raised flood curbs, equipment left unattended)
- Bumping hazards (e.g., low pipes)
- Operating machinery (e.g., rotating flywheels, turning belts, excessive noise)
- Fumes (e.g., carbon monoxide, natural gas, fluorocarbons)

A basic guiding principle is to always look up and down before moving into a mechanical area. Above all, *don't touch any of the equipment!*

TABLE 8.1	Mechanical Room Patrol Threat Assessment	
Problem Areas	**Area of Responsibility**	**Focus Points**
1 Mechanical room	Equipment/machinery	Low pipes Rotating fans Moving belts
2 Entrance to mechanical rooms	Door	Flood curb (tripping hazard)
3 Roof	Roof area	Roof edge Access door (you may not have keys to get back in) Wind
4 Containers	Top	Fluids
5 Electrical rooms	Transformer vaults	PCB exposure High-voltage relays
6 A/C room	Chiller	Loud noise (possible hearing damage)
7 Elevator penthouse	Cable mounting	Moving cable

What are you looking for?

In addition to looking for insecure mechanical areas and unauthorized persons, your primary task while conducting a mechanical room patrol is to identify any abnormal conditions (e.g., a fire or flood) that can result in damage to the equipment. Once identified, appropriate action must be taken that usually involves notifying an on-site building operator or an emergency contact. In extreme cases, power may have to be shut off.

The following is a brief list of some of the things to look for while conducting a mechanical room patrol:

Insecure Mechanical Rooms. Before locking the door, check to be sure contractors are not working in the area. You do not want to potentially lock them out of or in an area.

Unauthorized Persons. Unless you absolutely know the person (i.e., building staff) challenge *all* persons found inside mechanical rooms. For liability and security reasons they *must* be authorized. The time of day is also important. For example, the day porter being in an electrical room closet at 2:00 p.m. might be quite reasonable, but you might have some questions if you find that person there at 2:00 a.m. Internal theft of mechanical equipment and supplies (salt, sand, plywood, copper, etc.) is a real problem. Many justify their actions by stating, "Everybody does it." If someone is removing anything from a mechanical room, be sure they are authorized to do so.

Leaks and Floods. Water can cause a lot of damage in a very short period of time. Even a slow leak left unattended can cause extensive damage relatively quickly.

Defective Machinery. Know the "normal" sounds for all equipment operating within a mechanical area. High-pitched whining sounds may indicate the bearings are about to burn out in expensive machinery and the appropriate persons need to be notified right away. There are many cases of alert security staff reporting sounds that were not normal. Their actions have often saved the premises from thousands of dollars of damage.

Machinery Left Running. Building operators and engineers are human. They may forget to turn machinery off. *Do not turn on or off any machinery yourself unless you have been specifically told to do so by an authorized person.* When in doubt, check with your supervisor or management contact.

Gas Leaks. Natural gas is odourless, but gas companies introduce an odour in the gas to give it a distinctive smell. Go to the area where the gas metre is to get a whiff as to what this smell is. If you detect a strong concentration of that odour in an area, there may be a gas leak. Do not operate your radio or cause any type of spark. Immediately notify the Fire Department and keep well back from the area.

Fire and Safety Hazards. It is not enough just to report such hazards. You must take active steps to ensure the hazard is dealt with in a time frame that will not result in damage to the equipment or the site.

Use Your Senses

We have already addressed this issue before, but it is worth repeating. Use your senses during your patrols.

Look for any actual or potentially hazardous condition.

Listen for unusual sounds.

Smell the air for any gas smells.

Touch to feel for heat of a possible fire on the other side of a stairwell door.

PATROL ROUTE

For the most part, your patrol route will be dependant on the type of mechanical rooms in your building. In a typical commercial office building, mechanical rooms are located in the following areas:

Top Floor

- Air conditioning units
- Chiller
- Elevator penthouse
- Roof access
- Boiler room (it can also be in the basement level)
- Emergency generator

Each Floor

- Electrical rooms
- Telephone rooms (very sensitive – should always be locked, but will often be found unlocked in older buildings)

Basement/Garage Levels

- Sprinkler room
- Diesel room—check the exterior diesel intake valve (there should be a padlock on it to discourage vandalism/theft of diesel)
- Sump pump—used for movement of sewage/water
- Main electrical room

- Main transformer vault—your electric company has a key; generally, you won't
- Fire reset room

In many cases, you may have to take readings and note them on logs provided within the mechanical areas.

Boiler Room

Don't be surprised if the boiler flares up when you are walking by. It is just like your furnace— when there is a demand for heat (i.e., temperature drops below a certain point) one or more of the boilers will fire. You are looking for obvious problems in boiler rooms:

- Strong smell of gas
- Unnatural noises
- Floods
- Electrical problems (you don't want any electrical short-circuits in an area that may be exposed to residual natural gas)

Although the machinery may look interesting, *strongly resist the urge to touch anything or turn anything on or off. I can guarantee you will regret it if you do!*

Mechanical Penthouse

Chillers, fans, and other air conditioning, exhaust fans, return air fans, and circulating equipment are found in the mechanical penthouse. One of your primary concerns is leaks. If you notice a small leak on your first patrol, check on its condition on your next patrol. If the leak continues, follow your notification procedures. Be aware, however, that leaks may be classified differently from site to site. What would be considered a leak at one site would be seen as a flood in another. Leak tolerance will depend on several factors unique to each building environment. You must quickly learn what the tolerance range is. When in doubt, however, contact someone. The one time you don't, that small leak develops into a major flood and someone eventually asks, "How could you have missed this on your patrol? What were you doing?"

Sprinkler Room

Sprinkler rooms are generally located in the basement or garage areas. There are two sets of readings in the sprinkler room. One set measures the water pressure from the city as it comes into the building. The other set indicates the actual pressure of the building system.

There are two types of sprinklers:

Wet Systems. Water remains in the pipes under pressure right at the sprinkler head. These systems can only be used in areas where the temperature remains above freezing.

Dry Systems. Pressurized air is in the sprinkler pipe at the sprinkler head. For there to be a sprinkler discharge, water will have to flow to the head first. Dry systems are primarily used in underground garages where the temperature may dip below freezing.

Often, you will be required to take sprinkler readings on each of your patrols and record the values on a chart left in the sprinkler room. If the pressure falls below a certain point (due to minor leaks in the system), you may be required to "pump the system up" (an auxiliary pump is used to maintain water pressure). Clearly, you will only do this if you have been properly trained and instructed to do so. If you attempt to pump up sprinklers and open the valves in the wrong order, you can cause damage to the system. Sprinklers must be pumped up after a sprinkler discharge.

If the pressure drops below a certain "set point" value, the sprinkler alarm sounds and you will have to respond according to your specified instructions.

Roof Checks

Access to the roof must be severely restricted for liability and safety reasons. Roof access can normally be gained through a stairwell door at the top of the stairwell or via a mechanical room. On low-rise buildings, the roof can be vulnerable to attack. For this reason, the roof door may have a double lock. This can cause a problem for you if you gain access to the roof but, for some reason, can't use a key to get back. Before you go into an area, make sure you are able to get out of that area! You may think this is nothing to be concerned about.

Example

Your building has a lock on one side of a door leading into an atrium plenum. You can go through without a key but need a key to get back. That key was not included on your security ring. Thus, to check that area and get back, you would need to block the door open. On one occasion, you neglect to block the door open and become stuck in the plenum area. Fortunately, you have a radio and are able to radio the desk person to come up and "rescue" you. Can you imagine the predicament you would have been in had you not had the radio or there was nobody else in the building? These are things to think about because often, a Security Officer *will* be the only one in the building.

Check the roof for objects that may have been thrown up onto it. If you find something, determine appropriate action based on the object and your site policy.

Elevator Penthouse

The elevator penthouse contains the winches and electrical relays used for controlling the building's elevator system. With all the relays in the room, the temperature can become very warm. If the temperature goes above a certain point, the elevators will shut down as a safety precaution. This can happen during very hot summer days or if there is a problem with the building's air conditioning system. You may have to prop open the elevator penthouse doors to allow for air circulation. Fire and electrical hazards are the main points to look for in an elevator penthouse.

Sump Pumps

Occasionally, sump pumps break down and there is a sewage backup. There is generally an alarm on each sump pump that is activated if the water goes above a certain level. This alarm can be tested; the process would be described in your post orders if you are required to test the alarm. With respect to sump pumps, your main objective is to ensure they are functioning properly.

WHAT CAN YOU LEARN FROM BUILDING STAFF AND OUT-SIDE CONTRACTORS?

Security Officers are placed in a very unique position. They have access to all areas of the building and get to go into places that most people don't even know exist. As Security Officers gain experience, they will realize how much they can learn from the building operators and specialized contractors (i.e., elevator maintenance persons, HVAC repair persons, electrical contractors, etc.). Don't be a pest to them; you can learn a lot by observing and asking intelligent questions. You never know when that knowledge will be put to use in an emergency situation.

Although it is important for Security Officers to be curious about all operations of the building, they must never "experiment." You might think you can always correct something that you turned on "to see what happens" by turning it off, but this is not always the case.

Example

Where you work, loaded tractor trailers are parked in a compound. Part of security's job is to monitor the air conditioning reefer units to see which ones are on and which ones are off. The units turn on automatically depending on the set temperature for the load. One Security Officer who has a bit more curiosity than common sense takes it upon himself to "play" with the controls. He turns on a reefer unit that was supposed to be off. Because it was programmed, he wasn't able to turn it off! He notifies his supervisor but the client has to be notified to come and shut it off—at 2:00 a.m. Needless to say, the Security Officer was relieved early and without pay.

REVIEW QUESTIONS

Level A

1. Identify three crucial things you are checking for on a mechanical room patrol.
2. Why do you think the roof side of most roof access doors in high-rise buildings is not locked? Is this a potential breach in security?
3. What is the purpose of a flood curb in mechanical rooms?

Level B

1. Name at least six critical mechanical room areas you should check.
2. Why should telephone and electrical room closets be locked at all times?

Level C

1. You are working with a colleague who loves doing perimeter and mall patrols because she likes the "action," but she hates doing mechanical room patrols because she says they are "boring" and "unimportant." What would you say to her to change her mind?

Chapter 9

OFFICE TOWER PATROL

LEARNING OUTCOMES

At the conclusion of this chapter, you will be able to

- Relate officer safety considerations to conducting a floor-by-floor patrol
- Outline the specific functions of a floor-by-floor patrol
- Describe the abnormal conditions to look for while on patrol
- Describe appropriate theft prevention strategies based on incident analysis
- Establish an appropriate floor-by-floor patrol route

OFFICER SAFETY CONSIDERATIONS

In general, the office tower patrol, also known as the floor-by-floor patrol, is a lower threat level activity than the garage patrol, the perimeter patrol, and even the mechanical room patrol. The primary threat during office tower patrols is the potential threat posed by intruders in the office areas who are attempting to steal money and/or office equipment. Intruders may have either broken in or entered the office during hours of operation and hidden in an area (washroom, supply closet) until after hours.

Although the primary target of such intruders is cash and small, portable equipment such as computer laptops, *expect them to be armed.* They are not looking for a confrontation but, if challenged, you should expect resistance. Many are attempting to steal to obtain money to support a drug habit and you can expect them to be unpredictable.

TABLE 9.1	Office Tower Patrol Threat Assessment	
Problem Areas	**Area of Responsibility**	**Focus Points**
1 Washrooms	Cubicles	Hands
		Feet
2 Interior offices	Intruders	Hands
		Feet
		Weapons/objects seen
		Weapons/objects not seen

What are you looking for?

During office tower patrols, you are primarily looking for:

Insecure Office Areas. Some offices must be secure 24 hours a day, 7 days a week.

Intruders or Unauthorized Persons. Challenge all persons you find in the office or washroom areas after hours. If you do not know the person, ask for positive identification.

Safety and Fire Hazards. This includes coffee pots left on, short-circuiting electrical equipment, and desk lamps left on (overheating hazard).

Equipment Left On. Only turn off equipment you have been previously authorized to turn off. Much of the office equipment is automated now and will shut down after prolonged inactivity (e.g., photocopier). However, there may be equipment unique to your site that needs to be manually turned off.

Leaks and Floods. Pay close attention to kitchen and washroom areas, plumbing pipes, and upper mechanical areas (from where water may be leaking down). It is a good idea to have an instant or digital camera on-site to photograph any damaged areas. Photographs make for a more thorough report and can assist in documenting insurance claims.

Lights Left On. If nobody is in a lit area and you have the authorization to do so, it is prudent to turn the lights off. For this reason, you should always carry a flashlight when conducting office tower patrols.

PATROL ROUTE

There are a variety of different floor-by-floor patrol patterns you can use depending on the configuration of the building. If you also have an access control function, you will want to check the lobby periodically. Thus, you will only be able to check two or three floors at a time.

Alternating Floor-by-Floor Patrol or Combination Patrol

If you can access a floor via the stairwell, then the alternating floor-by-floor patrol is one of the best patrols to perform. You should conduct your patrol from the top floors down to the lower floors. Start at one floor, complete the floor patrol, and then use a stairwell to go down to the next floor. Complete that floor's patrol and then use a different stairwell to go down to the next floor. This type of patrol has the added advantage of combining a stairwell patrol spot check with a floor-by-floor patrol. As well, it introduces an element of surprise and randomness into your patrols.

Elevator Floor-by-Floor Patrol

If you cannot access floors via the stairwell, you will need to use the elevators to get to each floor. If you have to check the lobby periodically, it is not recommended that you patrol more than three floors at a time.

Areas to Check

In addition to any special areas that require patrol, you should check the following areas on each floor-by-floor patrol:

Electrical Rooms. Check for electrical short-circuits as well as improper storage of items in the electrical room. Too often, electrical rooms are used to store potentially flammable items. Document any such instances found.

Telephone Rooms. Although these rooms should be locked at all times, it is not unusual to find these rooms unlocked. In some cases, the locks are defective and the rooms *cannot* be locked. Such instances should be reported.

Lobby Areas. Make sure there are no unauthorized persons in the area.

Tenant Areas. If you have access, and you are authorized to be there, complete a check of the interiors of all tenant areas you have access to. You should check for unauthorized person(s) and safety/fire hazards within each tenant area you can access.

Information Security. Is confidential information readily accessible? (unlocked filing cabinets, computer terminals that are not password protected, confidential documents not shredded). Any, and all, such compromises should be documented via report.

Kitchen Areas. Check for coffee pots left on and leaks/flood coming from the coffee machine or sink area.

Above all, vary your patrol route as much as you can. Don't become predictable in your patrols. On certain days, you can randomly decide to increase the thoroughness on specific floors (this may be driven by incident history or it can be purely random).

Fire and Safety Hazards

Be very alert for any potential fire and/or safety hazards.

Fire Hazards

- Coffee pots left on
- Frayed electrical cord on cleaning equipment (vacuum cleaners)
- Improperly stored combustibles (e.g., paper strewn about)

Safety Hazards

- Tripping hazards (debris left in common areas, rugs bunched up—especially during winter months)
- Material filed above the safety height limit in filing areas

Insecure Office Areas

While the threat level may be lower in offices, there are still specific protocols that should be followed when you discover an insecure office area:

1. Check for signs of forced entry.

2. If it is evident there are signs of forced entry, *do not enter the area alone. Wait for backup from other security or the police.*

3. If there are signs of forced entry, record in your memo book all details pertaining to your discovery. Wait outside the area until the arrival of backup.

4. Once the area has been checked and all is found to be in apparent order, attempt to secure the area. Ensure the client contact has been advised, if notification is required within your post orders.

5. If it is confirmed that a break-in has occurred, notify the police and protect the crime scene until the arrival of police.

6. Complete and file a report documenting all details of the occurrence.

INTERACTING WITH OFFICE STAFF

As with the merchants in a retail mall, it is important you establish a working relationship with the office staff you are required to interact with to do your job. Listed below are critical people within any commercial office tower with whom you should be familiar and have an established working relationship:

Receptionists. They are your eyes and ears regarding what is going on in the building.

Mail Room Staff. You may be called upon to assist them with suspicious packages. It makes your job easier if you have previously made contact.

Cleaners and Day Porters. You should be asking them to let you know immediately if they spot anyone suspicious around the building.

Shippers/Receivers. They can be an excellent source of information pertaining to the movement of people and vehicles into and out of the building.

Maintenance Employees. They can tell you a lot about the building operations, and their advice can be invaluable when you are trying to solve a problem at 3:00 a.m.

Building Manager. They are your direct client and appreciate feedback from you regarding what is happening in the building.

THEFT PREVENTION

Most thefts from an office occur during the day, late afternoon, or early evening. As well, a large proportion of thefts are internal. The "usual suspects" are cleaners, building maintenance employees, and security staff. Often the thief proves to be an office staff member, however.

Crime can be effectively prevented through an understanding of The Theft Triangle shown in Figure 9.1 and described in Table 9.1. For a theft to occur, there must be motive, opportunity, and desire.

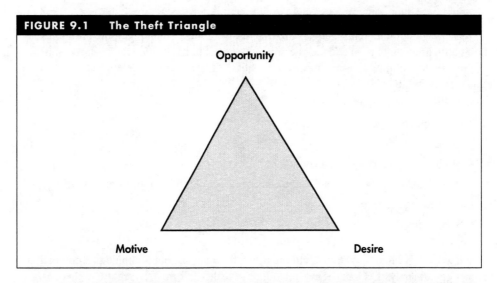

FIGURE 9.1   The Theft Triangle

Opportunity

Motive   Desire

TABLE 9.1   Components of The Theft Triangle

Component	Description	Prevention Strategy
Motive	There has to be some benefit to them in taking the item.	Fair compensation Benefits
Desire	They have to want to take it.	Prosecution strategy Clear recognition of consequence Expectation of being detected
Opportunity	They have to be able to take it.	Secure laptop computers Strict access control policy

Theft prevention must involve everyone, in every department, at every level. It is not something that can just be left to security. The most effective theft prevention strategy focuses on all three elements within the crime triangle. The crossover effects of prevention reinforce each other and make for a much more effective overall strategy.

Reporting Thefts

It is essential to ensure that all thefts and attempted thefts are reported to security and that a formal report on each is completed by security. All too often, thefts from vehicles are not reported because the individual calls police from home. Wherever possible, police should be advised of all theft incidents pertaining to a site. Police departments base their enforcement strategies, in large part, on reported incidents of crime. If reports of crime are low, then policing resources may be allocated elsewhere.

Theft Analysis

A formal crime prevention methodology can be used to analyze reported incidents of thefts. It uses a priority-setting matrix that comprises eight significant determiners characterized by:

priority, type of problem, magnitude, rate of change, fear index, loss value, system response, and reduction potential.[1] This analysis provides a clearer understanding of the problem and allows a focused strategy to address the concerns raised to be developed.

Prior to determining the priority-setting matrix, the problem statement must be stated clearly based on an analysis of:

- Target/victim characteristics
- Offender characteristics
- Time of the offence
- Modus operandi (how it was done)
- Spatial aspects (means of access, means of target identification, means of egress)
- Opportunity factors
- System response

We will not be able to go into detail regarding the analysis, but a sample of a completed security report analysis is located in Appendix B. Further information regarding this analysis technique can be obtained by referring to an excellent publication from the Solicitor General that is easy to understand and provides practical information that can be immediately applied:

Linden, Rick, Dr. 1994. *Crime and Incident Analysis for Community Policing.* Toronto, ON: Ministry of Supply and Services.

Sensitive Areas

Sensitive areas in a commercial office building include:

- Washrooms
- Crossover floors (stairwell doors are not locked on crossover floors)
- Insecure electrical closets and telephone rooms
- Mailroom
- Reception areas
- Shipping/receiving area
- Garbage compactor area
- Main lobby area
- Cleaning closets
- Mechanical areas
- Any area deemed sensitive based on past incident history

All sensitive areas should be identified within the site's post orders and each Security Officer should clearly understand his or her duties with respect to checking sensitive areas during regular floor-by-floor patrols.

Property Removal

Every building should have a formal property removal policy in effect that is communicated to all staff and enforced by all employees, not just security staff. When conducting floor-by-floor patrols, security must be very diligent when encountering anyone removing property contrary to the property removal policy. If everyone is aware there is a policy in place and it is being enforced, this will significantly reduce two legs of The Theft Triangle: opportunity and desire.

A formal documentation system should be in place that provides authorized property removal passes. All incidents pertaining to unauthorized equipment removal must be documented and followed up to determine the effectiveness and efficiency of the system.

Uncontrolled access/egress points should be monitored through Closed-Circuit Television cameras and/or intrusion alarm systems with on-site security response.

RESPONDING TO SERVICE REQUESTS

While on floor-by-floor patrol, Security Officers must be in a position to react and respond to requests for service. Notification for such requests can come through radio, or if there is a second officer on-site at a central access point, via pager, or via doorbell. When conducting single officer patrols, the Security Officer should not be away from the lobby for more than 15 minutes to avoid excessive waiting by persons requiring assistance.

Floor patrols are also an excellent means for security to interact with others in the building. By assisting others to the degree possible, security builds on the staff relationship network that is fundamental for an effective system of loss prevention. At all times, security must emphasize what they *can* do as opposed to what they *cannot* do.

REVIEW QUESTIONS

Level A

1. When conducting floor-by-floor patrols, why is it good practice to spot-check the stairwells while completing the floor check?
2. As a male Security Officer, would you check the female washrooms while conducting a regular floor-by-floor patrol? As a female Security Officer, would you check the male washrooms while conducting a regular floor-by-floor patrol? Give reasons for your answer.
3. What life-safety equipment, if any, would you normally check while conducting regular floor-by-floor patrols?

Level B

1. It is 5:00 p.m. and you are checking the receiving area. You notice an employee exiting the receiving area carrying a laptop computer. The existing access control and property removal policy requires all persons leaving the building to exit by the main lobby and that

a property removal pass be presented for all laptop computers removed from the building. What actions would you take?

Level C

1. Your building's property manager tells you that over the last three months, a large quantity of building materials and supplies have been disappearing from the mechanical storage area in P1, the first level of the underground parking. What further information would you request and what loss prevention strategy would you consider?

STAIRWELL PATROL

LEARNING OUTCOMES

At the conclusion of this chapter, you will be able to

- Relate officer safety considerations to conducting a stairwell patrol
- Outline the specific functions of a stairwell patrol
- Describe the abnormal conditions to look for while on patrol
- Establish an appropriate stairwell patrol route

OFFICER SAFETY CONSIDERATIONS

There are two principal safety hazards associated with stairwell patrols:

1. *Tripping Hazard.* The possibility of a misstep occurring if the Security Officer is tired, preoccupied, talking on the radio, or in pursuit of a suspect.

   Prevention Strategy:

   - Wear appropriate hard-soled, non-slip footwear.
   - When in the stairwell, focus on the task of ascending or descending the stairs.
   - Remain stationary while talking on the radio.
   - Keep one hand free to hold on to the guide rail.

- Exercise extreme caution when pursuing or speaking to a subject within the stairwell.

2. *Suspects.* Encountering subjects in the stairwell is potentially very dangerous due to space limitations, and tripping, falling hazards. The most dangerous position to be in is when the subject is farther up the stairs than you are.

Prevention Strategy:

- Walk *down* the stairs when conducting a stairwell patrol. You will be in the superior position if you encounter a suspicious person and the subject will have a default escape route. The worst thing to do is "corner" a subject.
- *Do not* interact with the subject on the stairs. For both your safety, and the safety of the subject, move to a stairwell landing.
- You should be in Condition Orange when approaching the subject.

TABLE 10.1 Stairwell Patrol Threat Assessment		
Problem Areas	**Area of Responsibility**	**Focus Points**
1 Stairwell landing	Intruder	Hands Feet Weapons/objects seen Weapons/objects not seen
2 Stairwell ground floor exit	Exterior door	Behind door
3 Top-floor landing	Intruder	Hands Feet Weapons/objects seen Weapons/objects not seen

What are you looking for?

While conducting stairwell patrols, you should be looking for:

Suspicious Persons. Stairwells serve as entry/exit paths and are often used by subjects while conducting a pre-attack survey. The very top of the stairwell and the very bottom of the stairwell under the landing are frequent locations where suspicious persons are found. Perhaps such persons think that security does not check those locations frequently. Look for evidence of recent occupation (burning cigarette butts, urine, empty bottles).

Suspicious Activity. Normally, people do not congregate in stairwells. If you encounter two or more persons loitering in a stairwell, you should establish why they are there. In many cases, it will be an attempt on their part to circumvent any smoking regulations in the building, but there may be other, more sinister reasons why they are in the stairwell. In apartment complexes, subjects can use stairwell landings as a staging area prior to an attack on an apartment (home invasion or gang attack).

Burnt-Out Exit or Stairwell Lights. Report on any burnt-out Exit lights.

Locked Doors. Check each stairwell door that is supposed to be secure to ensure it is secure. Check any insecure area following appropriate officer safety rules.

Stairwell Door Floor Numbers. Report on any stairwell doors where the floor numbers are peeling off or the painted numbers are faint and difficult to read. In an emergency, low light, or smoke filled condition, it is imperative the stairwell floor numbers be readily identifiable from the stairwell side. This is especially true for crossover floors. It is recommended that the numbers be red because the longer wavelength of this colour is more discernable in smoke conditions. Stairwells should be uniquely identified both on the stairwell side and on the floor side (e.g., Stairwell #4 or North Stairwell). Security suggestions should be made if any of the appropriate signage is deficient.

Suspicious Packages or Objects. Frequently, subjects either deliberately or accidentally leave stolen merchandise in a stairwell or under stairwell landings because they had been surprised or intend to come back for it later. For example, an office employee might furtively place a laptop computer in a stairwell during the day in hopes of returning after hours to retrieve it. If a suspicious package is found, follow the procedure as described in Chapter 13, Bomb Threats.

Insecure Stairwell Doors. In a fire situation, it is critical that stairwell doors close completely to provide a protected escape route within the stairwell. As you go by each landing, hold the door open to a 45° angle and release the door. The door should close completely and form a tight seal with the door frame. If it does not, file a report as this is a safety hazard. This only applies to stairwell doors you can access, are not alarmed, and you are authorized to access.

PATROL ROUTE

Stairwells can be patrolled in one of two ways:

1. *Complete Patrol.* Where a single stairwell is patrolled from top to bottom.
2. *Combination Patrol.* Where the stairwell patrol is combined with the floor-by-floor patrol.

The choice of patrol will depend on the Security Officer's purpose. If the purpose is entirely focused on the stairwell, the complete patrol should be chosen. If the purpose is a patrol of the entire complex, the combination patrol should be chosen.

When starting the stairwell patrol, the Security Officer should always start at the top level and walk down. Go to the very top of the stairs, quietly open the stairwell door and *listen* for the sounds of anyone in the stairwell. If you remain quiet, activity in the stairwell can be detected almost down to the ground level (depending on the number of floors). Even if just doing a complete patrol, the Security Officer should open the stairwell door at each landing and briefly listen for any sounds of activity on the floor.

Alarmed Areas

Sensitive floors may have alarms installed on their stairwell doors (these doors may also be locked). Be aware that some alarms are so sensitive, even lightly pulling on them will activate them. These are special considerations you should be aware of *before* starting your patrol. It is embarrassing to have tugged on the door, set off the alarm, and then have to explain your actions to responding police or alarm response operatives. To ensure these very sensitive doors are secure, a light pull or a visual check to ensure the door is secure and in line with the frame is sufficient.

Crash-Bar-Only Doors

Be particularly wary of doors that only have the crash bar on the floor side and no handle on the stairwell side. You may be tempted to not bother checking this type of door because it "looks" secure. Often the crash bar may not have caught and by lightly pulling on the door with your fingertips, it will open. Sometimes, suspects will deliberately plug the striker plate to prevent the door from securing. Typically, this type of door exits directly from a tenant area and is thus particularly sensitive.

REVIEW QUESTIONS

Level A

1. Why is it important from an officer safety perspective to walk down a stairwell when conducting a stairwell patrol? (Compare this to walking up an underground garage stairwell.)

2. State three specific hazards to watch for while conducting a stairwell patrol.

3. State what a crossover floor is and what its life safety function is.

Level B

1. On your first stairwell patrol, you consistently find a brick blocking open the ground floor stairwell exit that goes out into the receiving area. What are some possible reasons why this door is being propped open? What recommendations would you make to your supervisor to address this issue?

2. Why is it important to conduct the stairwell door test to ensure each stairwell door will close completely and securely on its own?

3. Explain in detail the different types of stairwell patrols and indicate under what circumstances you would use each type.

Level C

1. Your property manager has asked you to prepare a presentation on life safety and theft prevention for the tenants in the building. A number of small, petty thefts have been occurring on every floor during the day, and two weeks ago, tenants on the second floor complained of nausea. It was later found that the second floor, north stairwell door and the ground floor north stairwell exit (which exits out to the receiving area) had been blocked open and fumes from a truck idling in the receiving compound had entered the stairwell. From a review of incident reports over the past month, you noted the following:

   • 8 reports indicating stairwell doors were found blocked open during the day (these were on floors where the stairwell opened directly into tenant areas)

- 4 door maintenance reports indicating stairwell doors did not close properly
- 2 reports that stairwell door floor numbers were missing from crossover floors
- 6 alarm reports indicating someone had gained unauthorized access to the stairwell

What would be your recommendations to the property manager? What would you say to tenants? Submit this as a formal report.

ORDER MAINTENANCE PATROLS

LEARNING OUTCOMES

At the conclusion of this chapter, you will be able to

- Relate officer safety considerations to conducting an order maintenance patrol
- Define order maintenance patrol
- Describe the abnormal conditions to look for while on patrol
- Identify appropriate strategies and tactics to apply to this type of patrol

OFFICER SAFETY CONSIDERATIONS

An *order maintenance patrol* is a patrol conducted by two or more Security Officers to enforce the Trespass to Property Act in relation to specific prohibited activity on or in relation to a client property.

TABLE 11.1	Order Maintenance Patrol Threat Assessment	
Problem Areas	**Area of Responsibility**	**Focus Points**
1 Parking lot	Vehicles	Front and rear bumper Open door Rolled down window Open trunk
2 Parking lot	Persons	Hands Feet Weapons/objects seen Weapons/objects not seen
3 Food courts	Persons	Hands Feet Weapons/objects seen Weapons/objects not seen
4 Washrooms	Cubicles	Hands Feet
5 Roof area	Roof edge	Thrown objects

Threat Level

Typically, order maintenance patrols have the highest threat level and should always be conducted by a minimum of two or more highly trained, well-equipped, and experienced Security Officers. For most patrols, company policy and client requirements do not allow Security Officers to patrol in pairs unless they are doing so as part of a training or briefing requirement. The exception is order maintenance patrols where a minimum of two officers are required to provide appropriate contact and cover when conducting their assigned tasks.

Reasons for Order Maintenance Patrols

A client may request order maintenance patrols for a variety of reasons including:

Chronic Loitering Problem

- A strip plaza that does not have regular security coverage
- A food court where a large influx of abnormal users frequent that area at specific times
- Washrooms where sexual assaults or frequent incidents of inappropriate behaviour occur

Backup to Existing Security

- Site Security Officers that are overwhelmed by abnormal users
- Site Security Officers that have been attacked/assaulted by abnormal users

Previous Incident

- Response to a previous serious incident (homicide, armed robbery, sexual assault, sexual predator activity)
- To reassure normal users on the site

New Security/Management

- New security service provider takes over an account where the previous security had been lax or intimidated by abnormal users

- New management may request the patrol for a limited period prior to instituting, or phasing in, longer term security coverage

In general, Security Officers are not perceived as specific targets. Security Officers conducting order maintenance patrols become specific targets when they directly try to initiate a behavioural change in abnormal users who frequent the area. For this reason, Security Officers on such patrols must continually operate at a Condition Orange or Condition Red level. As such, individual Security Officers should not conduct these patrols for more than two to three hours at a time.

Specific threats Security Officers may face include multiple suspects, suspects with weapons, vehicles, hostile crowds, and trained attack dogs.

What are you looking for?

The essential nature of order maintenance patrols is preventive. This type of patrol attempts to prevent further problems by effecting a change in the behaviour of, or displacing, abnormal users. The intent is not to "make arrests" or "show them who is boss," but rather to improve the actual and perceived comfort level for normal users of the property.

Equally important, such patrols are not meant to usurp the normal police role, but rather to supplement it. In fact, paid duty Police Officers frequently work with security in an order maintenance function. Such liaisons are frequently most effective and solve problems rather quickly.

While conducting order maintenance patrols, you should be looking for:

Loitering. Groups or individuals remaining in an area that has been specifically identified with "No Loitering" signage. The definition of loitering is subjective. However, experienced Security Officers will focus on the behaviour of the individuals and invoke the applicable section of the Trespass to Property Act to affect the desired behavioural change or displacement (i.e., individuals act in accordance with the owner's wishes or they leave). Look for groups or individuals frequenting a sensitive area and interfering with normal users' use of that area (i.e., washrooms, food courts, mall entrances, store entrances near arcades, etc.). Look for groups or individuals remaining in their vehicles parked in an area that has been signed for a specific purpose (e.g., "Parking Is for the Use of the Convenience Store Customers Only.")

Suspicious Persons/Activities. All subject approaches should be conducted using the contact/cover principle.

Disturbances. Security Officers may choose to disengage and call for police backup.

Gang Members and Gang Activity. All intelligence relating to gang members and gang activity should be collected and, where there is an existing liaison, shared with the appropriate police agency. When dealing with bona fide gangs, it is imperative that police be available to directly assist on-site security due to the high degree of potential danger.

Criminal Activity. When criminal activity is observed, appropriate notification should be made to the police.

PATROL ROUTE

There is really no predetermined patrol route for Security Officers conducting order maintenance patrols. The routes chosen will depend on the nature and purpose of the patrols. Such patrols may be random or pre-set, depending on the purpose. Officer safety considerations must always be taken into account when the routes are planned. For example, for high-threat residential patrols, Security Officers would not want to needlessly expose themselves to attack by objects thrown from high-rise units. The patrol route would be planned to maximize their aerial cover.

Prior to commencing coverage, the security representative responsible for establishing the operational requirements of the route should discuss the above considerations with the client and/or police and establish a preferred route based on the desired strategy and purpose of the patrol.

SPECIAL EQUIPMENT AND TRAINING

Not all security companies are in a position to safely and effectively provide order maintenance patrol coverage and not all Security Officers are capable of, or have the desire to, conduct order maintenance patrols. The following are suggested minimum requirements with respect to equipment and training for those engaged in order maintenance patrols:

Equipment
- Protective body armour (mandatory)
- Handcuffs (recommended)
- Side-handled batons (suggested)
- High-profile uniform (recommended)
- Plastic disposable gloves (mandatory)
- Protective gloves (suggested)
- Access to first aid kit (mandatory)
- Vehicle (optional – depending on the nature of the coverage. Many types of order maintenance patrols are conducted by mobile operatives that are able to "time share" with a variety of properties)
- Flashlight (mandatory)
- Radio/cellular telephone (mandatory – you must be able to immediately contact the police for assistance)

Experience and Training
- Minimum of one year security experience (preferably in a retail mall environment or at any type of site that requires frequent interaction with the public and involvement in arrest situations)
- Minimum of a two-year law and security administration or police foundations diploma from a recognized college or equivalent
- Training and certification to carry an approved side-handled baton
- Use of force and advanced defensive tactics training

- Exposure to tactical ground fighting and spontaneous knife defence training
- Exposure to an approved crisis intervention training program
- Demonstrated knowledge of the Criminal Code and Trespass to Property Act
- Certification in first aid and CPR (ideally, level C)
- Demonstrated ability in report writing

In addition, such Security Officers should not have displayed any attitude or deportment during their training or prior work performance that indicates it would not be in the interest of public safety to allow them to work in such an environment.

POLICE LIAISON

The effectiveness of any order maintenance patrol depends, in large part, on the degree of co-operation Security Officers have established with police. Ideally, the police should be advised prior to the establishment of any such patrols. Also, where possible, input from the police should be reviewed when establishing the patrols.

Security Officers should ask police about area demographics; area crime statistics; documented incidents of attacks on police or security in the area; general building and area conditions; and specific officer safety concerns on-site Security Officers may have raised. Police should be advised of all major incidents relating to the patrols and they should also be advised once the patrols stop.

THREAT AND VULNERABILITY ASSESSMENT

Figure 11.1 indicates the relationship between threat and vulnerability in relation to who should be conducting order maintenance patrols.

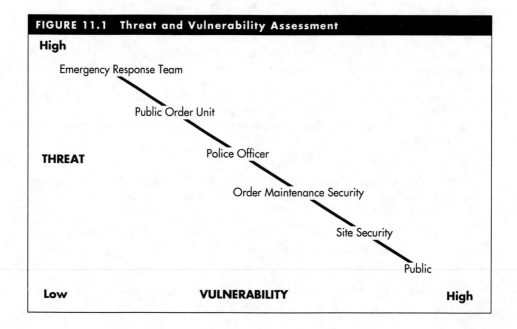

FIGURE 11.1   Threat and Vulnerability Assessment

A specific threat and vulnerability continuum should be established for each order maintenance assignment. Security Officers must be prepared to continually assess the situation and if they find they are approaching the limit of their acceptable range, they should disengage and contact police for assistance in dealing with the situation.

STRATEGY AND TACTICS FOR DEALING WITH ABNORMAL USERS

For the most part, abnormal users who create situations requiring the deployment of order maintenance patrols operate on the basis of the "psychology of intimidation." Security Officers conducting order maintenance patrols must adopt a system of strategy and tactics that successfully removes abnormal users' reliance on such intimidation. One of the more effective strategies is to speak directly to abnormal users. By talking with them as individuals, you remove part of their "group identity" and make them accountable as individuals. Any intelligence that can be gathered regarding the names, aliases, street names, and gang affiliations is very useful to security. For example, when speaking to a group of individuals, by referring to individuals within the group by their first name, you put them on notice that they will be directly accountable for any criminal acts they may become involved in. This can have a remarkable calming affect.

REVIEW QUESTIONS

Level A

1. What is an order maintenance patrol?
2. What conditions may cause a client to request an order maintenance patrol?
3. Why do order maintenance patrols potentially have the highest threat level?

Level B

1. Distinguish between "threat" and "vulnerability." Give examples of each.
2. Identify five desirable behavioural traits someone involved in order maintenance patrols should have. Identify five undesirable traits someone involved in order maintenance patrols should not have.
3. *Criticality* refers to the impact an event may have on an entity, business, or individual. For our purposes, we can assign the criticality of an event a value from 1 to 5 according to the following scale:

   1 = Fatal to the business, entity, or person

   2 = Very serious (major impact on balance sheet or a person's well-being)

   3 = Moderately serious (noticeable impact)

   4 = Relatively unimportant

   5 = Seriousness unknown

Based on the above scale, assign a criticality to the following five possible events you may encounter during an order maintenance patrol:

A = You encounter an individual who refuses to speak to you or acknowledge your presence.

B = Your vehicle side window is smashed in retribution for an arrest you made.

C = The wheel bolts are loosened on one of the tires on your vehicle in retribution for an arrest you made.

D = You face the prospect of assault charges arising from an encounter with an individual where it is alleged you used excessive force.

E = Five individuals refuse to move out of your path to allow you and your partner access to the building lobby.

Discuss your reasons for assigning a particular value to each possible event.

Level C

1. How receptive do you think most Police Officers are to the idea of private security conducting order maintenance patrols? Discuss.

TIMED CLOCK ROUND PATROLS

LEARNING OUTCOMES

At the conclusion of this chapter, you will be able to

- Define timed clock round patrol
- Outline the advantages and disadvantages of this type of patrol
- Identify how audit results can be used

DEFINITION OF TIMED CLOCK ROUND PATROLS

A timed clock round patrol (formerly referred to as a "detex patrol" in reference to the standard punch clock traditionally used by security) comprises specific locations that must be visited by security. A magnetic bar or some other identifier is affixed to each location. The Security Officer carries a device that records his or her visit to the location (a key is inserted in a lock, a "wand" is swiped, etc.). A hard copy or electronic record is generated that verifies the date, time, and punch location. These patrols may be done in random order or in a specified order depending on client requirements. Advanced monitoring devices allow the Security Officer to punch in codes on the unit he or she holds that records specific items found (i.e., door/window found open, etc.).

Why are they necessary?

Certain types of clients (e.g., government, institutions) require absolute proof that a security check was conducted at a specific location, on a certain date, at a certain time. Insurance requirements may also dictate a similar requirement.

Timed Clock Round Patrols: Advantages and Disadvantages

Advantages

- They provide documented evidence that a specific location was visited by someone at a specific date/time.
- They ensure that security, or someone, is attending each of the specified locations a prescribed number of times during a shift.
- They create an audit trail of all security activities on-site.

Disadvantages

- They only ensure that "someone" visited the location. They do not guarantee that someone was the Security Officer (i.e., a friend or other on-site worker could have completed the round for the Security Officer).
- They do not ensure that the Security Officer looked at anything, only that he or she visited the location. The tendency is to focus on completing the "clock patrol" and not on patrolling for the sake of observation purposes.
- They are potentially demoralizing to security staff. In effect, their managers are saying to them, "We don't trust you to do your job."
- They can establish a patrol routine that others may use to their advantage. "Oh, the Guard is off on his detex round. We can break into this area now. He won't be back for another 20 minutes."
- They encumber the Security Officer with further items to carry that may create potential officer safety concerns.
- They detract from the total survival mind-set because they potentially encourage the Security Officer to remain in Condition White.
- They perpetuate the "Security Guard" stereotype of a minimally competent, poorly educated, poorly paid individual who can't even be trusted to walk around the work site every few hours.

There are some security companies, that, for the reasons described above, absolutely refuse to accept contracts where their Security Officers are required to conduct clock rounds. On the other hand, there are other security companies who take the position that the client is paying for a service and it is not their role to pass judgment on the value of that service. Ultimately, it is up to each individual Security Officer to decide whether he or she will work for a company that requires the completion of clock rounds.

With the widespread use of programmable access cards, a permanent electronic record is created that verifies card use and access to particular locations as the Security Officer conducts the patrol. An audit trail is established and, with the widespread use of Closed-Circuit Television cameras, positive identification can be made of usage. Use of such cards has none of the disadvantages of the traditional clock rounds and yet an audit trail is created.

REVIEW QUESTIONS

Level A

1. What is a timed clock round patrol?
2. Give examples of where verification from a clock round could be of benefit to
   - The security organization
   - The client
   - The Security Officer

Level C

1. Using the Internet, or other source, research the use of clock rounds in security.

   (a) What company first established clock rounds?

   (b) What was the origin of the word *detex*?

   (c) Identify some of the current products that make clock round patrols possible.

BOMB THREATS

LEARNING OUTCOMES

At the conclusion of this chapter, you will be able to

- Outline the 3P approach to dealing with bomb threats
- Explain the primary effects of explosions
- Use the Bomb Threat Checklist
- Explain a two-person floor-and-room search

THE 3P APPROACH TO DEALING WITH BOMB THREATS

A bomb threat can create panic and disorder in any business or establishment. The key to successfully dealing with a bomb threat is to follow the 3P approach:

- Planning
- Preparation
- Practice

Planning

An emergency plan must be prepared to deal with bomb threats and as a minimum, *must* include:

1. Procedures for Receiving a Bomb Threat
   - Completion of Bomb Threat Checklist (see Figure 13.2)
   - Notification
   - Assessment of the threat

2. External Support
   - Prior contact should already have been made with police, fire, and ambulance personnel. In some jurisdictions, the emergency plan itself must be reviewed by emergency services personnel.
   - A procedure must establish protocol for notification of external agencies in the event of the receipt of a bomb threat. Security must know who notifies external agencies, the criteria for notifying them, and the criteria for not notifying them.

3. Search Procedures
   - The procedures must be documented and established in advance with each search team already predetermined (see Figure 13.3).

4. Actions
When a suspicious package or object is found
   - Do not touch it.
   - Notify your command and control centre.
   - Relay the following information to command and control:
     (a) Location of the object
     (b) Reason it is suspicious
     (c) Description of the object
     (d) Any other useful information
     (d) The most direct route to the object
   - Command and control will
     (a) Ensure perimeter control is established to prevent anyone from approaching the object or attempting to move it.
     (b) Notify the authorities.
     (c) Ensure someone familiar with the area meets the authorities to direct them to the area.
   - Other searchers will
     (a) Continue searching their assigned areas for a bomb until all have reported in.
   - It is recommended that you
     (a) Open all windows and doors near the area to allow ventilation and minimize blast damage.
     (b) Place sandbags on adjacent walls to avoid blast and shock damage.
     (c) Tape or cover window glass with canvas or tarpaulin to prevent damage from exploding glass.[1]

5. Evacuation Procedure
   - Establish *who* authorizes the evacuation.
   - Establish *how* the occupants are advised.
   - Establish *where* they are to go.

Preparation

All employees must receive training according to their expected degree of involvement in a bomb threat response. A four-tiered training model is described in Table 13.1.

TABLE 13.1	Bomb Threat Training Model		
Level	**Who**	**Need to Know**	**How**
1	All employees in the building	Evacuation procedure	Seminars Drills (2x year) Employee orientation
2	Floor wardens, search teams	Search techniques	Emergency procedures Monthly meetings Drills (2x year)
3	Security, building operations staff	All activities required of them during the emergency	Training checklists Performance evaluations Shift briefings Drills (2x year)
4	Security manager	Emergency planning	Disaster recovery Seminars Conferences Formal training

Practice

Emergency drills should be carried out at least twice a year. Where possible, local authorities should be notified and invited to participate.

Why are bomb threats serious?

Bomb threats are serious for three fundamental reasons:

1. Danger of human injury/death due to bomb explosion and/or possible reaction from fear/panic of bomb threat (stampede to exit)
2. Damage to structure (includes physical damage and economic loss due to closure)
3. Total costs involved include
   - Idle work time
   - Lost wages
   - Reduced productivity
   - Uneasiness and anxiety[2]

All of the above must be considered when designing a countermeasure—any activity that is implemented to reduce the risk of injury to persons and/or loss or damage to property. The single most important countermeasure is effective control over the entry of personnel and material into the building.[3]

TYPES OF EXPLOSIONS

There are three basic types of explosions:

1. Mechanical
   * Heat and pressure gradually build up inside a closed container until the increased pressure shatters the container and there is a rapid escape of gas. An example would be an exploding pressure cooker.
2. Chemical
   * This type results from the rapid conversion of a solid or a liquid into gases with much greater volume.
   * This type is accompanied by extremely high temperature and pressure.
   * It creates smoke and noise.
3. Nuclear
   * It results from the fission or fusion of nuclei under pressure.[4]

Primary Effects of Explosions

There are three primary effects of an explosion: blast, fragmentation, and incendiary/thermal.[5]

1. *Blast.* The term *brisance* refers to the shattering power of an explosion. When an explosion detonates, the expanding, hot gases form a shock wave.

   A blast has two phases. Phase 1 is the *positive phase* when gases are expanding outward. Phase 2 is the *negative phase* (or implosion) when gases return to fill the partial vacuum created by the expansion. This phase is less powerful than the positive phase but three times as long.
2. *Fragmentation.* This effect is the breakup of the original container. Fragments are expelled outward at speeds up to 2 700 ft./sec. (823 m/sec.).
3. *Incendiary/Thermal.* This effect depends on the type of explosion. High explosives have a velocity greater than 3 000 ft./sec. (914 m/sec.) and produce a higher temperature than low explosives.

Figure 13.1 clearly shows the primary effects of an explosion and the positive and negative phase of the shock wave:

Figure 13.1   Primary Effects of an Explosion

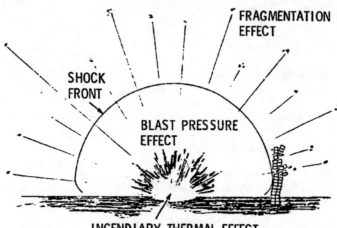

FIGURE 1
Three primary effects produced by the detonation of an explosive — (1) blast pressure,
(2) fragmentation, (3) incendiary or thermal

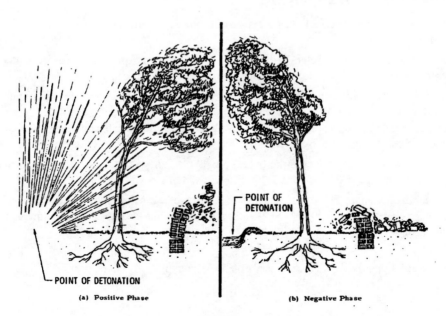

FIGURE 2
Positive and negative phases of an explosion

Source: From *The Protection of Assets Manual*, POA Publishing, 2000.

FREQUENCY OF ACTUAL BOMBS

In the United States, the Treasury Department Bureau of Alcohol, Tobacco & Firearms (BATF) has a team of highly trained specialists who belong to the National Response Team. This team is dispatched to U.S. bombing incidents. The unit was formed in 1978 and for the period from 1978 to 1993, it reported:

- 283 responses to bomb threats
- 259 deaths due to bombs
- 1 913 injuries due to bombs
- US$1.7 billion in property damage due to bombs.[6]

DELIVERY AND PLACEMENT OF BOMBS

Bombs can be delivered to premises through four primary means:

1. Person
   - Worker, visitor, service person, delivery person, solicitor, etc.
2. Object
   - Purse, handbag, briefcase, or anything that can be carried in by a person
3. Mail
4. Vehicle or Conveyance
   - Largest and most dangerous explosions are from vehicles as a larger bomb can be delivered (e.g., World Trade Centre)[7]

Placement of the device depends on the attacker's nerve and local site knowledge. Any of the following areas are potential areas where a bomb could be placed:

- Washroom
- Janitor's closet
- Stairwell
- Telephone room
- Electrical closet
- Garbage room
- Shipping/receiving area
- Tenant- or owner-occupied interior space
- Lobby area and hallway
- Elevator
- Internal mail conveyance system
- Ventilator or A/C duct.[8]

RECEIPT OF AND RESPONSE TO BOMB THREATS

Acceptable protection from bomb threats depends on an adequate access control system, not on a threat response.[9] There are three steps to a threat response:

1. *Analysis.* Estimating the need for response
2. *Decision.* Choosing what to do:
    -   Nothing
    -   Full search
    -   Partial search
    -   Partial evacuation
    -   Full evacuation

    It is recommended that searches be undertaken after bomb threats are received. This will help to remove the premises from liability and ensure maximum protection. Evacuation should only be done if a suspicious device is found or there is a strong reason to believe the threat is real (e.g., known terrorist organization making the call).
3. *Implementation of Response Decision*[10]

Bomb Threat Analysis

Credibility

-   Time of day and day of week
-   Mode (telephone, mail)
-   Specificity of threat (time, place, etc.)
-   Identity of caller (child, female, male, young, old)
-   Possibility of access to area for placement of device

What is the proper response?

-   Ignore warning?
-   Conduct limited search of specific area?
-   Conduct general search?
-   Conduct limited or general evacuation?

How is the response implemented?

-   PA, telephone, cascade system, messenger?
-   Who/where evacuated?
-   Who/where searched?
-   Who will notify law enforcement and emergency services?
-   What should be done if something suspicious is found?
-   What is "something suspicious"?
-   If people are evacuated for how long?
-   Who will determine when to return to normal operation?[11]

Bomb Threat Checklist

All persons who may answer a telephone should have a copy of the bomb threat checklist nearby to allow them to quickly refer to it and complete it as they are talking to the caller. Figure 13.2 represents a typical bomb threat checklist.

FIGURE 13.2   Bomb Threat Checklist

INSTRUCTIONS:
- **A copy of this checklist shall be kept near all telephones capable of receiving outside calls.**
- **Keep calm. Do not get excited or excite others.**

Time Call Received			Time Call Terminated	

EXACT WORDS OF THE CALLER: (Use back of form if more spaced required)

QUESTIONS TO BE ANSWERED

a	When is the bomb set to explode?					
b	Where is it located?		Floor		Area	
c	Type of bomb?					
d	Description					
e	Reason for planting bomb?					
f	Who is calling?					

DESCRIPTION OF VOICE

Male		Female		Calm		Nervous	
Young		Old		Middle aged		Rough	
Refined		Accent		Intoxicated			

Speech Impediment? (Describe)

BACKGROUND NOISE

Music		Running Motor (type)		Traffic	
Whistles		Bells		Horns		Aircraft	
Tape Recorder		Machinery		Other	

ADDITIONAL INFORMATION

a	Did caller indicate knowledge of the building?				
b	What line did the call come in on?				
c	Is the number listed?		Unlisted?		
d	Is this a night number?		If so, whose?		

Date:		Name (Print)	
Signature		Position	

Searching the Premises

If a search is conducted, the following points should be considered:

- The search should be conducted in two-person teams.
- The search should be conducted by those very familiar with the area of the search.
- Searchers should keep visual contact during the search but should maintain maximum physical separation.
- Searchers should know the exact procedure to follow if suspicious packages are located.

Room Search Protocol

For maximum thoroughness, the following approach is recommended:

1. Divide the area of search into four height regions: waist to floor, eye level to waist, ceiling to eye level, above ceiling level (i.e., above a false ceiling).
2. Each searcher should switch roles and redo the complete room search checking over each other's area.
3. Check all cabinets, drawers, or any area in the room that is reasonably accessible.
4. Check above the false ceiling.

If a suspicious object is found:

1. Don't touch it.
2. Move back to a safe vantage point where you can prevent others from approaching the object, but are as far from it as possible.
3. Notify your command and control centre by telephone, *not* by radio.
4. Follow command and control's instructions.
5. Do not use a radio at any time because the radio frequency generated may trigger the detonator of an explosive device.

Figure 13.3 is a standard diagram showing a two-person room search following a standard search pattern. This diagram may appear somewhat complicated, but it is a very simple process to follow once it is applied. The path followed by both searchers is a standard "space filling curve" that is subject to three constraints:

1. Maximum distance must be maintained between both searchers at all times while searching.
2. The entire area of the room must be covered.
3. The room must be searched in a minimum time frame.

FIGURE 13.3 Two-Person Room Search

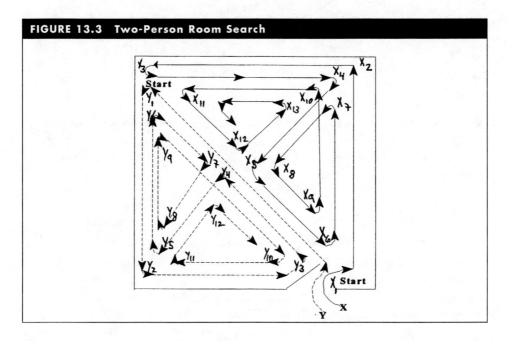

Step	Who	Action
1	X	The search starts at corner X1 next to door and follows path X1–X2.
1	Y	Y goes directly to far corner of room and starts search at Y1 along path Y1–Y2.
2	X	When areas next to wall have been searched, X then moves to corner X4 and begins to search towards centre X5.
2	Y	When areas next to wall have been searched, then Y moves to centre of room at Y4 and searches towards corner Y5.
3	X,Y	Both continue to search each of the four room quadrants following the path as indicated in the diagram.

Note: The distance Xi–Yj must be the maximum distance at each step. X and Y must move in synchronization and not get ahead or behind of each other.

Constraints

You want to maximize the area searched and minimize the time taken subject to the constraint that X_i–Y_j remains a maximum value.

Floor Search

The floor is searched in the same manner with X and Y starting at opposite ends and maintaining a maximum separation at all times.

REVIEW QUESTIONS

Level A

1. Define brisance.
2. What is the single most important countermeasure strategy to follow when dealing with bomb threats?
3. Why is it not a good idea to evacuate every time a bomb threat is received? (List five plausible reasons.)

Level B

1. How do you determine if something is suspicious? Give two or three examples.
2. Is the command and control centre always established in the lobby or security office? Explain.
3. Contrary to what should be done in a fire, it is a good idea to open up windows and doors to an area where a suspected bomb is. Why?

Level C

1. Why do people make bomb threats? Plant bombs?

14

ACCIDENTS

LEARNING OUTCOMES

At the conclusion of this chapter, you will be able to

- Identify the types of accident situations you may be called on to deal with
- Establish your response priorities
- Identify specific response requirements depending on the accident situation

ACCIDENT ASSISTANCE

As a Security Officer you will be called upon to assist accident victims. Whether someone is the victim of a slip and fall, an industrial accident, a vehicular accident, an assault or other criminal act, or a medical emergency (e.g., choking on food), the person sees a Security Officer in a uniform and expects assistance. It makes no difference to the person whether you are a Police Officer or an ambulance attendant, he or she sees the uniform and wants immediate assistance. Are you up to the challenge?

Response Priorities

Your basic priorities as a Security Officer at an accident situation are to

Protect Life. Given the choice of preserving someone's life through the immediate application of first aid or pursuing and arresting the person that stabbed them, you *must* always provide assistance first to someone in a life-threatening situation. The only exception would be if the offender was still at the scene and presented an immediate threat to you, the victim, or others in the area.

Preserve the Scene. As a first responder, you are directly responsible for preserving the scene until the arrival of police or other emergency personnel. In general, don't touch things at the scene. The exception might be weapons you may have to secure to prevent them from being used against you. Where possible, leave the scene undisturbed.

Protect Property. As you would in a first-aid scenario, you must prevent the situation from becoming worse. Your mandate as a Security Officer is to "protect people, property, and information." Clearly, you must protect your client's property to the best of your ability. This also extends to the property of the victim, once the other priorities have been attended to, and to the property of anyone on the scene.

Identify Witnesses. At the very least, obtain the name, address, and telephone number of any witnesses. They might not wait for and may be reluctant to speak to the police. If possible, attempt to keep witnesses separated from each other so their independent versions of the events can be relayed to the police.

Apprehend Any Offenders. Providing all the above priorities have been met and it is safe to do so, and you have the lawful authority (i.e., it is a "found committing situation" where you saw the offender committing a criminal act), arrest the offender and turn him or her over to the police.

Document the Details. Record in your memo book all information pertaining to the occurrence, including arrival times of all emergency services; names, addresses, and telephone numbers of any witnesses; a brief sketch of the scene; and unit and badge numbers of any attending Police Officers. It is also your obligation to prepare a witness statement, if requested by attending police. Be aware that your witness statement may be used at any criminal, civil, or coroner's inquest arising from the incident. Your witness statement must be factual and describe your direct knowledge and your actions relating to the occurrence. It is not appropriate for you to include information not directly relevant to the event (e.g., indicating there were supposed to be two Security Officers on duty, but there was only one). This is secondary information that will be followed up by police or other investigators depending on the relevance and severity of the incident. As well, you wouldn't include comments such as "I told management in the past about these problems. They never listened to me or did anything."

SLIP AND FALL ACCIDENTS

Traditionally, a *slip and fall* refers to any accident that occurs to a patron resulting in his or her falling on the property. The cause of the fall may have been his or her own negligence or a contributing environmental factor (e.g., snow, ice, water on the floor). The procedure described below would be the same for any other type of personal injury accident on the property (e.g., a person walks through a glass window).

It is critical that you

- Respond promptly.
- Provide emergency first aid.

- Take action to prevent any further injuries by others (e.g., if there is a patch of ice outside mall doors, ensure maintenance sands/salts it or blocks the area off).

- Investigate the incident fully. This will involve speaking to the victim, witnesses, and photographing/sketching the area.

- Write a full report. This report may be used by your client to form part of the statement of defence if the victim undertakes civil action.

Specific information you will require regarding slip and fall accidents includes:

Victim Information. Include the name, address, telephone number, and age of the victim.

Witness Information. Include the name, address, and telephone number of each witness.

A Brief Description by the Victim of What Happened. If they can write it out for you, much the better. Depending on the severity of the accident, you may not be able to obtain this information because the victim may be unconscious or you are continuing first aid until the arrival of an ambulance. Management representatives or the property's insurance adjusters would normally follow up with the victim later. Whatever information you can get from the victim at the scene is vital because it is the best evidence you can get on the event. Caution: A person's recollection of events may be temporarily blocked out by the shock of the occurrence and it is always important to cross-reference the victim's description of events with independent witnesses.

Description of Any Prior Medical Condition of the Victim. A prior condition may have contributed to the accident (e.g., they were on crutches, they already had a broken arm). Specific categories include: not applicable, physically challenged (specify), intoxicated, emotionally disturbed person.

Footwear the Victim was Wearing. This can be a crucial point for later liability as inappropriate footwear the victim was wearing may have been a contributing factor (e.g., hard-soled shoes with no rubbers on a winter day or excessively worn shoes that caused a misstep). If possible, examine the shoes and, if available and it is convenient to do so, take a photograph of them. At the very least, describe the footwear in detail and note any unique identifying marks on them. Describe wear patterns on the shoe. *If you can, on your own time, speak to a cobbler about footwear to learn some of the terminology and how you can describe wear patterns.*

Clothing the Victim was Wearing. Provide a detailed description.

Objects the Victim Was Carrying at the Time of the Accident. Examples are briefcase, parcels, cellular phone, etc.

Weather Conditions at the Time of the Accident. You should note weather conditions in your memo book at the start and finish of your shift and update your memo book when weather conditions change during your shift.

Surface Conditions of the Area Where the Victim Was Walking. Was the surface clear, dry, snow covered, wet, ice covered, normal, under construction? Again, sidewalk and parking lot surface conditions should be noted in your memo book as you do weather conditions.

Surface Type of the Area. Was it smooth concrete, uneven concrete, asphalt, tile, soft earth, hard packed earth, grass, etc.?

Emergency Services. Record the unit number, name(s)/badge number(s) of any attending emergency personnel.

Disposition of the Victim. Was he or she treated at the scene by ambulance staff, transported to hospital (get the name of the hospital)?

Description of Any Visible Injuries of the Victim. Also note what the victim says he or she feels (e.g., "My leg feels broken. My arm is numb.")

Contributing Factors. Identify any possible contributing factors to the accident (e.g., possible inattention due to victim observed talking on a cellular phone prior to the accident, wet floor "Caution" sign knocked over or stolen, bright sunlight, darkened area). Be very careful of what you record. Make sure it is direct evidence and not your opinion. What you write down may be used against the property owners. That is not to say you don't make notations, but only note the facts you observe. Don't offer opinion.

Preventive Actions

You can take a number of steps towards preventing slips and falls in the first place or at least reducing the premise's liability.

Watch for Safety Hazards

Watch for safety hazards while on patrol. A tripping hazard is posed by a crumpled up doormat, snow/ice buildup, spills on the floor (e.g., liquid, ice cream), unsafe behaviour (e.g., little children climbing up on planters), very large planter gratings (i.e., people can fall down them). Where possible, immediately correct the problem by straightening the doormat, advising parents of the unsafe actions of their children. Parents do not always welcome comments about their children, but you have an obligation to caution them. If it is not possible for you to correct the situation, report it to maintenance and either remain at the scene until it is corrected or ensure the area is properly blocked off. Document all safety hazards encountered by yourself and the steps you took to rectify them. This documentation establishes due diligence and can be invaluable in preparing a statement of defence against civil claims.

Know the Occupier's Liability Act

Obtain a copy of the Occupier's Liability Act from Publications Ontario (1-800-668-9938/(416) 326-5300) to gain a better understanding of your obligation, and the property owner's obligation, regarding the standard of care expected for persons who may be on your property. The cost of the act is minimal and is well worth the investment.

Know about Risk Management

Consider taking supplemental courses in risk management through your local college or university. Much of the material in these courses can be directly applied to your site.

Get Information from Your Insurance Adjuster

With your client's—and company's—permission, invite your property's insurance adjuster to give a brief presentation to you and your staff on the various proactive strategies that can be implemented to reduce liability claims. Insurance adjusters will also give you the specific requirements of reports.

VEHICULAR OR CONVEYANCE ACCIDENTS

When investigating vehicular or conveyance accidents, much of what was written above is applicable. It is critical that you establish the following points:

Injuries. Identify who is injured and the nature and extent of the injuries. This information must be relayed to attending emergency services.

Involved Parties. Identify the drivers: Who was the driver of the blue car? Identify any passengers: Who was the passenger on the black motorcycle? Don't make assumptions. Not all injured parties will let you know. They may very well be in shock. As well, parties can be ejected a fair distance from their vehicle. Emergency staff have documented cases of attending an accident scene and coming across victims in fields a fair distance from the vehicles.

Witnesses. Include the name, address, and phone number of each witness. Briefly describe what they observed.

Attending Emergency Services Personnel. Include the unit numbers, names, and badge numbers of attending personnel. Don't be a pest about this and interfere with their activities but make sure you get the required information before they leave. You will need it for your report. Include the time you arrived on location and the times emergency services called, arrived, and departed.

Involved Vehicles. Remember to *complete a description of all involved vehicles.* Include a description of the damage and damage estimate to involved vehicles. Complete driver information, including insurance company and policy/expiry number (very important if there was any damage to the site property).

Sketch/Photographs. Make a sketch of the accident scene in your memo book and, where possible, take or obtain photographs.

Directing Traffic

You may be called upon to direct traffic at an accident scene on your property or for special events on your property. Remember: You have no authority on a public roadway.

When directing traffic you want drivers to understand four things:

1. That *you* are the officer who will tell them what to do
2. When to stop
3. When to go
4. When to turn

Position yourself in a central area where drivers will see you. Make sure you are wearing a reflective vest. If lighting conditions are poor, you should be using a coned flashlight.

How to Stop Traffic

1. Point with your arm and finger at the vehicle you wish to stop.
2. Once the driver notices you, hold up the palm of your pointing hand in the universal "Stop" position.

3. Repeat this action with traffic coming in the other direction.
4. Make sure you only try to stop a vehicle that has a reasonable chance to stop. You don't want to cause an accident.

How to Start Traffic

1. Position yourself with your side towards the car you wish to start.
2. Point with your arm and finger at the driver of that car.
3. Hold that position until the driver notices you.
4. Bending at the elbow only, swing your arm with the palm up towards your chin. Repeat this motion until the driver starts.

How to Have Drivers Make a Right Turn

1. *When* a vehicle approaches on your right, *then* point with your right arm to the driver.
2. *When* the driver notices you, *then* swing your arm over to the direction he or she is to go.
3. Keep pointing until the driver begins to turn.
4. *When* a vehicle approaches on your left, *then* point with your left arm to the driver.
5. *When* the driver notices you, *then* swing your left arm over to the direction he or she is to go.

How to Have Drivers Make a Left Turn

1. You may have to stop traffic in the lane(s) through which the vehicle will have to cross.
2. *When* a vehicle approaches on your left, *then* give the stop signal with your right arm to traffic in the lane that vehicle will have to cross.
3. Hold the stop signal with your right arm and give the turning gesture to the driver with your left arm.
4. *When* a vehicle approaches on your right, *then* turn around and face the direction the vehicle is to go.
5. Stop traffic with your right arm and give the turning gesture with your left arm.

It is *critical* that drivers and pedestrians know what you want them to do and when you want them to do it. As well, it is important you use the same standardized hand signals that drivers and pedestrians have come to expect.

Signalling aids such as a whistle can be useful to get the driver's attention:

- One long blast = Stop
- Two short blasts = Go
- Three short blasts = *Wake up!*

Minor Vehicular Accidents

For minor vehicular accidents that don't require the presence of the police, you should obtain full driver information from all involved parties (name, address, phone number, insurance information) and a complete description of all involved vehicles including licence number and damage. As well, note any property damage and include a sketch/photograph. You may wish to remain until the drivers have exchanged information in case one of the drivers becomes assaultive towards the other or attempts to flee the scene. Ensure there are no injuries. Complete and file a report documenting all of the above information.

Many jurisdictions have a collision reporting centre where drivers go to report minor accidents. Make sure you know the address, telephone number, and specific location of the nearest collision reporting centre.

INDUSTRIAL ACCIDENTS

Treat industrial accidents as you would any emergency situation focusing on the priorities mentioned above. With respect to industrial accidents, it is important that any machinery not be turned back on and that the area be protected for follow-up investigation by the Ministry of Labour if there has been a serious injury or fatality involving a worker. Police will often notify Ministry of Labour investigators if they respond to a serious industrial accident.

There is a reporting obligation on the part of building management, but they normally take care of any notification requirements, providing you have properly advised them via report and on-scene notification.

Needless to say, you must complete and file a report on the accident.

DOCUMENTATION AND FOLLOW-UP

Make sure all documentation you submit is in accordance with your company and site policy. As well, keep in mind the points regarding documentation in Chapter 4.

At times, you may not have received all required information at the time of the incident (either because you forgot to ask for it or the party was not available). When police are involved, an important follow-up piece of information is the police occurrence number assigned to the incident. You may wish to follow up with the Investigating Police Officer to obtain the occurrence number.

Following Up and Releasing Information

If you have to contact people by telephone, make sure you place your calls during business hours and clearly identify who you are and the reason for your call. Many sites have a policy that only the supervisor, director, or management representative can make such follow-up calls. At times, you may also receive calls asking for follow-up information. Do not release any information unless you know it is the Investigating Police Officer looking for follow-up information, or you have been specifically authorized by management to release the information. Refer such calls to building management or to your supervisor.

REVIEW QUESTIONS

Level A

1. Identify the main type of accident situations you may be tasked with responding to as a Security Officer.
2. What specific hazards and officer safety concerns would you have in attending to a serious vehicular accident on your property? State at least five.
3. Why is it important to be able to describe the footwear worn by someone involved in a slip and fall accident?

Level B

1. After a major accident, a news reporter approaches you and states she "would like to take your picture because of the excellent way you handled the situation" and that, "off the record" she would just like to have you describe to her what happened. What would your response be?
2. Identify some potential industrial accidents that could occur:
   - In a commercial office building
   - In a retail mall
   - In an industrial plant
3. While speaking to you about a fatality that occurred on your property, the Investigating Police Officer starts asking you questions about your company's training process, what the staffing levels on the property should be, and other questions not directly related to the accident. How would you respond?

Level C

1. With reference to the Occupational Health and Safety Act, identify and discuss the key reporting requirements of an accident.

CRIME SCENE PRESERVATION

LEARNING OUTCOMES

At the conclusion of this chapter, you will be able to

- Define what a crime scene is
- Establish your priorities when dealing with a crime scene
- Understand the importance of crime scene sketches
- Understand the legal consequences of being involved at a crime scene

SECURITY OFFICERS AND CRIME SCENE PRESERVATION

Security Officers are often at a crime scene prior to the arrival of police. It is critical they understand their role in protecting a crime scene.

A *crime scene* is any situation that has arisen from the commission of a serious criminal offence and includes all physical evidence relating to the offence. It can extend beyond the immediate area of the occurrence (i.e., path of entry/exit of suspect, victim, etc.).

Common Crime Scenes

Some examples of common crime scenes are

- Parking lots where a murder, rape, or serious assault occurred
- Vehicles where a murder, rape, or serious assault occurred
- Interiors and exteriors of premises where a break and enter occurred

As the first or second Security Officer arriving at a crime scene, you have various responsibilities at a crime scene. Table 15.1 lists these responsibilities in order of priority.

TABLE 15.1	Priority Actions of Security at a Crime Scene	
Priority	**Action**	**Response**
1	Protect people.	Protect your safety and that of your colleagues and any persons in the area.
2	Render first aid.	Render first aid to the degree you are qualified to do so.
3	Preserve the scene.	Protect and preserve the crime scene.
		Do not touch or examine items or allow others to do so. Ensure any weapons are secured.
		Do not walk through the area.
		Do not smoke, drink, or eat anything in the area.
4	Record information on, and possibly arrest, the suspect.	Record any spontaneous utterings (e.g., "I didn't mean to kill him.")
		If you have the authority to do so (i.e., you saw the offence take place) and it is safe to do so, and it is in accordance with your company's policy and training, arrest the involved suspect.
		At the very least, record a detailed description of any suspect(s), including any weapons involved and the last known direction of travel of the suspect(s).
5	Record information on, and possibly help, the victim.	Record a detailed description of the victim. Do not touch the victim unless required to render first aid (i.e., don't go looking for ID, etc.).
		Record the name, phone number, and address of the victim, if available.
6	Record information on the witnesses.	Record the name, phone number, and address of each witness.
		Ask witnesses to remain until the arrival of police.
		Don't ask witnesses to describe the occurrence in detail, but if they start talking, write down what they say.
		Keep witnesses separate.
7	Take photographs.	If a camera is immediately available, take pictures of the crime scene.
		Record in your memo book the date, exact time, location, and photo number of any pictures taken.

(Starting from the first picture taken, negatives are clearly numbered).

Note: Unless you have a camera readily available, you probably won't be able to take any photos immediately before the arrival of the police. As well, expect the police to ask you to turn over to them any photos you take that can provide material evidence.

8	Record emergency response arrival and departure.	Record the exact time of notification, arrival (and departure), unit numbers, and badge numbers of any emergency units that arrive.
		Make sure you record the name and badge number of the first Police Officer on-site as that officer assumes responsibility for the crime scene.
		Quickly brief the officer on what you have done.
		Follow the instructions of the Police Officer.
9	Document the details.	Fully document all details of the crime scene and your actions. You may be called five or six years later to give evidence at a civil proceeding, criminal trial, or coroner's inquest.
		Draw a rough sketch of the crime scene in your memo book. This sketch will prove invaluable months or years later if you are asked to give evidence.
		Complete a formal company/client report as required.
		Record any spontaneous utterings or dying declarations of victim or suspects.
10	Make statements to police only.	Do not make any statements to the media or anyone else.
		The only person(s) you should give a statement to are Police Officers if they request a witness statement.
		Remember, you only describe what you actually observed and did in the witness statement.

Formal Crime Scene Sketch and Photographs

Once police have cleared the crime scene, and subject to your own abilities and the policy of your client and company, either you or your supervisor should prepare a detailed crime scene sketch with high-quality photographs attached. See Figure 15.1 for a sample crime scene sketch.

This follow-up information will not likely be used in any criminal matter (the "best evidence" is your notes and memo book sketches made at the time), but it may prove very useful to the client's insurance adjuster/lawyers in providing a defence for any civil litigation arising out of the occurrence.

FIGURE 15.1   Crime Scene Sketch

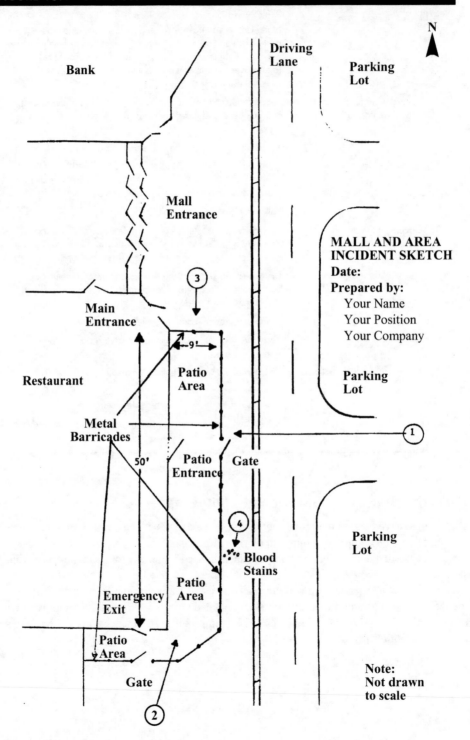

Figure 15.1 shows the degree of detail normally required for a formal crime scene sketch. Again, it is understood that such a sketch would only be prepared after the police investigation has been completed and with the approval of your client and supervisor. Such sketches are not difficult to create, but they do require a detailed examination of the area and extensive measurements. Photographs will prove invaluable. For those lacking photographic experience, your local school or community college will often offer introductory classes in photography that provide the basic skills required for your purposes.

Note: If you do not feel confident to prepare a formal crime scene sketch, then do not prepare one on your own. Use the brief sketch completed within your memo book, or enlist the assistance of someone capable of preparing a crime scene sketch.

At a minimum, any crime scene sketch should include

- A scale and detailed measurements
- A legend clearly identifying any symbols used
- A geographic directional arrow
- The date and full address of the location of the crime scene.
- The name, title, and position of the person(s) who prepared the diagram.
- Standardized symbols for vehicles, traffic lanes, etc. (templates can be purchased through any police/security supply store)
- All details relevant to the incident with specific areas referenced in your detailed memo book entry (everything noted in the crime scene diagram should be referenced in your memo book)

CIVIL LITIGATION

Regardless of how thoroughly and professionally you have done your job, it is becoming more commonplace in Canada for victims (or their families) to launch civil action suits against the property owners when serious incidents have resulted in death or injury.

For example, a victim is murdered by a suspect in a mall parking lot. The suspect is apprehended by security and held for police. First aid was unsuccessfully provided by security to the victim. Security acted in a professional manner and did everything they possibly could. Yet the victim's family still sue the suspect, mall owners, security company, and responding Security Officers. The family alleged negligence on the part of the security company due to lack of training of its staff, negligence on the part of the owner due to improper lighting, negligence on the part of the Security Officers (e.g., they dealt with the suspect earlier and directed him to leave the property, but failed to ensure that he or she left).

Punitive and exemplary damages arising from such a lawsuit can be in the millions of dollars. As well, punitive damages are generally not covered by insurance. Even if each party is only held liable for a small percentage, the amount still can be hundreds of thousands of dollars. Security Officers may feel fortunate if they or their company is not named directly in the lawsuit, but the client/property owner can still file a cross-claim against Security Officers and their company. This is often done on the client/property owner's part to reduce direct liability. This puts Security Officers in an awkward position, especially if they had reported defects/concerns to their client prior to the incident and nothing had been done.

It is imperative that security do their job in an unbiased, professional manner. Equally important, they must document what they have done. For example, if a Security Officer provides employee safety/security shoplifting seminars or invites police to give such seminars, he or she must be sure to document the day/date and who attended such events. This information may be critical when he or she is asked to provide information to the client's lawyer or insurance adjuster to assist in preparing a statement of defence.

As a result of thorough documentation, many third-party liability cases are stopped at examination on discovery when the plaintiff's lawyer realizes they do not have a likely chance of winning. At the very least, they may be prepared to settle for a smaller amount. Remember, however, the standard for civil cases is "balance of probabilities" not "beyond a reasonable doubt" as is required for criminal matters.

Giving Evidence in Court

At some time during their security careers, most Security Officers will be called on to give evidence in court. For many, this can prove to be a very traumatic and unpleasant experience. It need not be. If Security Officers have done their job professionally, have fully documented the incident, and are willing to truthfully testify to the best of their ability as to what they saw and did, then appearing in court can be a very significant learning opportunity.

Notification

When Security Officers are required to give evidence in court relating to matters arising from incidents that occurred while they were on duty and working at a client property, they will normally be served with a witness subpoena either at their personal residence, their place of work, or their company's office. The witness subpoena specifies the date, time, and location where the officer is to appear. As well, the name of the accused, the specific charge, and any material item(s) the officer is required to bring with him or her are also noted on the witness subpoena. When served with a witness subpoena, a Security Officer should immediately notify his or her supervisor/manager and, if requested, provide a copy of the subpoena to the appropriate management representative within the company.

Most security companies have a process in place that outlines the steps to take after being served with a witness subpoena. As well, this process will also indicate the type and amount of compensation officers will receive for their time spent in court. This is something a Security Officer should check prior to accepting employment with a company. It is too late to find out after you have been served with a witness subpoena that your company will not reimburse you for your time spent giving evidence in court.

Note: Failure to appear in court after being served with a witness subpoena can result in a fine and/or imprisonment.

Preparation

If the date/time noted on the witness subpoena conflicts with other scheduled events that the Security Officer cannot change (e.g., a prepaid, out-of-country vacation) then the Security Officer should immediately contact the investigating officer to discuss the situation and see if the trial date can be rescheduled. As well, the Security Officer should confirm with the Investigating Police Officer exactly what items should be brought to court. At the very least, the Security Officer should take with him or her the memo book where the incident was documented.

Prior to the court date, the Security Officer should assemble all the required items to be taken to court. Shift schedules may also have to be rearranged to ensure the Security Officer's shift will be covered to allow him or her to attend court.

Deportment

Security Officers should be in uniform or suitable business attire when attending court. It is important that officers look their best and present an appropriate professional appearance because they represent both their client and their security organization.

Outside the Court

Subject to time constraints, the Crown attorney may wish to speak briefly with the Security Officer prior to court commencing. For this reason, it is recommended the Security Officer attend court at least one-half hour prior to the time specified on the witness subpoena. When attending court, the Security Officer should be very careful about what he or she says and does. The accused and/or the accused's defence attorney could very well be waiting on the benches outside the courtroom or be in the public washrooms. A Security Officer does not want to say, or do, anything that may detract from his or her professional demeanour. Do not discuss the incident in a public area. If the defence attorney approaches you outside the court and wishes to speak to you, advise him or her that you would want to speak to the Crown attorney or the Investigating Police Officer before you could answer his or her questions.

Giving Evidence

Make sure you attend the proper courtroom. Verify on the trial list outside the courtroom that you are at the proper location. Sometimes, courtroom numbers change from what you were originally advised on the subpoena. On entering the courtroom go to the court clerk (who will be at a desk in front of the judge's bench) and identify yourself. Show the clerk your witness subpoena to verify why you are there. Turn off any pagers and/or cellular telephones while in the courtroom.

When giving evidence, it is important to keep in mind the following:

- Don't guess. If you don't know the answer to a question, say you don't know.
- Speak in a normal tone of voice and at a pace that allows the judge to keep up with you. He or she will be taking notes.
- Always ensure the judge and/or jury can hear what you are saying.
- Ask the judge for permission prior to referring to your memo book to refresh your memory.
- Answer all questions to the best of your ability. If you don't understand the question, ask for clarification.

- Remain professional and, above all, don't lose your cool. You are not on trial, the accused is.
- Do not step down from the witness box until excused by the judge.
- Do not leave the courtroom unless excused by the Crown attorney as you may be required for cross-examination.
- Prior to leaving the courthouse, attend the fees office to present your witness subpoena to ensure you receive your witness fees.

REVIEW QUESTIONS

Level A

1. Define what a crime scene is.
2. State the top five priorities when responding to a crime scene.
3. How far can a crime scene extend? How far would you reasonably be expected to control a crime scene?

Level B

1. State three limiting factors that affect your ability to control a crime scene.
2. When drawing a crime scene sketch for your purposes, should it be drawn to scale? Why or why not?
3. State two reasons why your property management may not want you to draw crime scene sketches.

Level C

1. A fatality has occurred on your property and you are dutifully protecting the crime scene until the arrival of police. A vehicle shows up that appears to be an unmarked police car. Two persons exit and walk over to you. They show badges and identify themselves as detectives. You look at your watch and start to write down their names in your memo book. One of the detectives speaks to you:

Detective: What are you doing?

Security: I'm writing down your name and badge number and the time when you arrived.

Detective: Don't do that. Wait until the other officers arrive. We'll let you know if we have been here or not.

How would you respond? What would you do?

C h a p t e r

16

FIRE AND LIFE SAFETY SYSTEMS

LEARNING OUTCOMES

At the conclusion of this chapter, you will be able to

- Identify the critical components of a building's fire and life safety system
- Distinguish between wet and dry sprinkler systems
- Explain The Fire Triangle
- Explain the steps for effective fire prevention
- Identify the four classes of fire

FIRE AND LIFE SAFETY SYSTEMS

Security Officers require a working knowledge of the fire and life safety systems at their site. Specific instructions are normally provided in the site's post orders regarding security's duties in using the fire and life safety systems. The following brief overview outlines the systems Security Officers may expect to encounter.

The type of fire and life safety systems at your site will depend on the age of the building and on the nature and size of the building. Each municipality has specific fire and life safety codes that buildings must comply with. Some of these regulations may not apply to older buildings, however, and would only be applicable if structural changes are made to the buildings. A building's fire and life safety system usually comprises the following:

Fire Detection System

- Heat sensors
- Rate-of-rise detectors (detect rapid change in temperatures)
- Ionization detectors (detect fire in the pre-ignition stage)
- Smoke detectors
- Manual pull stations

Fire Suppressant System

- Sprinkler system
- Fire hoses
- Fire extinguishers

Fire Alarm System

- Fire alarm panel (often the fire alarm system will be monitored off-site by an alarm monitoring service)
- Alarm bells (warn occupants in the building that an alarm has activated)

Smoke Exhaust System

- When a fire alarm is activated, the building's air circulation shuts down to prevent the spread of smoke throughout the building. For buildings that have a smoke exhaust system, the system will take air from the building and blow it outside through a series of smoke hatches.

Elevators

- During an alarm state, elevators will automatically shut down, or are manually called down by security, except for one or two elevators that are placed on fire service for use by firefighters.

Testing

All of the building's fire and life safety equipment must be tested on a regular basis. Specific instructions in each site's post orders generally clarify the role of site security in this function.

Sprinkler Systems

Sprinkler rooms are generally located in the basement or garage areas. There are two sets of readings in a sprinkler room. One set measures the water pressure from the city as it comes into the building. The other measures the actual pressure of the building system. There are different types of sprinklers:

Wet Systems. Water remains in the pipes under pressure right at the sprinkler head. These systems can only be used in areas where the temperature remains above freezing.

Dry Systems. Pressurized air is in the sprinkler pipe at the sprinkler head. For there to be a sprinkler discharge, water has to flow to the head first. Dry systems are primarily used in underground garages where the temperature may go below freezing.

Dump Systems. Dump systems are generally used in restaurants or other food preparation areas. They are installed directly above the grills and when activated, will "dump" a fire suppressant directly onto the grill area. Activation can be either manual or through a heat sensitive monitoring device.

In many cases, you will be required to take sprinkler readings on each of your patrols and record the values on a chart left in the sprinkler room. If the pressure falls below a certain point (due to minor leaks in the system), you may be required to "pump the system up" (there is an auxiliary pump that is used to maintain water pressure). Clearly, you will only do this if you have been properly trained. If you attempt to pump up sprinklers and open the valves in the wrong order, you can cause damage to the system. Sprinklers also have to be pumped up after a sprinkler discharge. If the pressure drops below a certain "set point" value, the sprinkler alarm will sound and you will have to respond according to your specified instructions.

The Fire Triangle

For a fire to occur, three elements must be present:

1. *Fuel.* There has to be something present that will burn.
2. *Heat.* There must be a source of ignition.
3. *Oxygen.* It is required to support combustion.

These three elements together form The Fire Triangle in Figure 16.1.

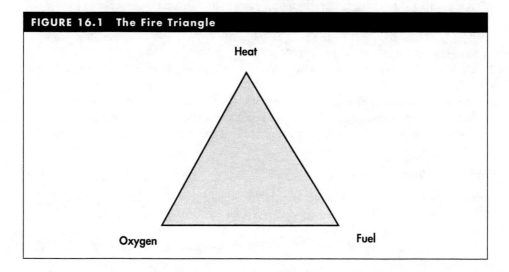

FIGURE 16.1   The Fire Triangle

Heat

Oxygen

Fuel

Remove one or more elements in the fire triangle and either a fire will not occur or an existing fire will be extinguished. This strategy has been applied effectively from a fire prevention perspective and is the basis for fire suppressant technology.

Classes of Fires

Table 16.1 summarizes the four classes of fires and how they can be extinguished.

TABLE 16.1	Classes of Fires	
Class	Description	Extinguished by
A	Ordinary combustibles (e.g., paper, wood, cardboard)	Water – It removes heat and cools material to below the ignition point.
B	Flammable liquids (e.g., gasoline, oil, grease)	Carbon dioxide, foam, sand, or earth – They remove oxygen through a "smothering" action.
C	Electrical fires	Carbon dioxide, foam, or dry powder – They remove oxygen through a "smothering" action. Do not use water due to the conductive nature of water.
D	Burning or combustible metals (e.g., magnesium, potassium, sodium)	Dry powder – It removes oxygen through a "smothering" action.

It is critical that all Security Officers be aware of the different classes of fires and what should be used to extinguish them. As well, every Security Officer should know the location of all fire extinguishers and should receive some training regarding the proper use of fire extinguishers. Fire extinguishers should be checked regularly by Security Officers to ensure they are present (many fire extinguishers disappear prior to the Victoria Day weekend for use in boats, cottages, etc.); they are fully charged; and access to them is free and unobstructed. Should any of the above not be the case, the Security Officer should immediately report the matter to his or her supervisor for follow-up.

Although a formal inspection process should occur monthly, Security Officers should get in the habit of checking fire extinguishers during their normal patrols—at least ensuring they are present and fully charged. On an annual basis, the entire fire and life safety system should be completely checked by a qualified service company. All such records of inspection should be maintained for the appropriate period (normally seven years for legal purposes).

Fire Prevention

Security Officers should always maintain a vigilant attitude when it comes to fire prevention. Situations Security Officers should be on the lookout for while conducting their patrols include:

Smoking in Unauthorized Areas. Always enforce existing non-smoking policies. They are usually in place for a reason.

Accumulation of Combustible Material. Examples are wooden pallets outside shipping/receiving areas; cardboard left in back corridors; and improper storage of material/equipment in electrical rooms or other inappropriate areas.

Defective Equipment. For example, frayed cords on electrical equipment such as vacuums could create a potential electrical short-circuit.

Coffee Pots Left on and Unattended. Historically, this used to be a significant fire hazard. Newer machines have more safety features, but should still be checked for malfunctions.

Christmas Tree Lights. Many fires have resulted when such lights have been left on over an extended holiday period, especially if a live tree is used.

Electrical Equipment Left Running and Unattended. Overheating may result.

This list is by no means exhaustive but is meant to give Security Officers examples of what to look for. Each property, or site, will have specific challenges Security Officers should be made aware of during their initial briefing tour. Always play the "what if" game while on patrol. For example: What if an electrical short-circuit occurred and ignited the cardboard stacked too closely to it?

Fully document all hazardous situations. Where appropriate, you should take direct action to prevent a fire from immediately occurring (e.g., turn off the coffee maker, move the cardboard), or report the situation immediately to a management representative. Do not make the mistake of ignoring the situation because, "It's always been like that," or "Nothing has ever happened before." When it comes to fire prevention and life safety, you cannot afford to take the risk.

REVIEW QUESTIONS

Level A

1. State five components that would normally be part of a building's fire and life safety system.

2. Why is it important for elevators to ground and not be used when a fire alarm is activated?

3. Why would you not find a wet sprinkler system in the garage?

Level B

1. Why is it important for Security Officers to have a working knowledge of their building's fire and life safety system?

2. How could you use your normal patrols to test a portion of the fire and life safety system?

3. Would Exit lights and the building's emergency generator system be considered part of the fire and life safety system? Why or why not?

Level C

1. Prepare a sample checklist that could be used by Security Officers on patrol to check portions of the building's fire and life safety system they would normally be responsible for testing.

17

ACCESS CONTROL SYSTEMS

LEARNING OUTCOMES

At the conclusion of this chapter, you will be able to

- Identify the three general components of any system of countermeasure
- State the 4D approach to access control
- Identify the various levels of access control
- Understand how CCTV systems can assist security

COMPREHENSIVE ASSET PROTECTION

Proper design and implementation of an asset protection program uses the systems approach: "comprehensive solution to a total problem."[1]

There are three general components to any system of countermeasure:

1. Vulnerability Analysis

   How vulnerable is the premise to attack or compromise? Vulnerability is determined by the physical environment and usage patterns.

   Example 1: A premise that has poor or non-existent locks on the perimeter doors has a high vulnerability to attack.

Example 2: A premise that has an elaborate system of locked doors, mag-locked areas, and alarm sensors is still vulnerable if users prop doors open to go to their cars, have a smoke break, etc. Alarms don't stop people from gaining unauthorized access.

2. Countermeasure Selection and Installation

   People. Security Officers, receptionists, etc.

   Hardware. Physical barriers, locks, safes, vaults, etc.

   Software. Written policies and procedures, training programs, etc.

3. Operating System Testing

   Regular tests of the operating system should be made according to an established schedule and certainly no less than annually.

The 4D Approach to Access Control

Access control is an asset protection system that incorporates all three elements of effective countermeasures: people, hardware, and software. Effective access control incorporates the 4D approach:

Deter unauthorized persons from attempting to gain access.

Detect when breaches to the access control system occur.

Delay unauthorized persons from gaining access to critical areas.

Detain unauthorized persons (police or security response).

People, hardware, and software must be carefully planned to ensure that all three interact positively and economically to increase the overall protection of the facility.[2]

Examples

1. A well-trained, motivated security force (people) does not deliver optimum protection if it is not properly equipped with radios, memo books, access to communications, etc. (hardware) or is not provided with documented policies and procedures (software).

2. A system with excellent physical security (e.g., CCTV system and intrusion alarms) does not provide optimum protection if there is nobody available to respond.

Why should Security Officers know about access control?

From a patrol perspective, an understanding of access control is important for two reasons:

1. The Patrol Officer may be required to provide breaks for the person permanently assigned to the access control point.

2. Patrol Officers are required to react and respond to access control breaches and it is important they understand significant features of the system and its inherent limitation (e.g., a camera that is not properly focused).

Access Control Continuum

A continuum scale demonstrates the various levels of access control. Aspects of each level can be used singly or in collaboration. Ultimately, the effectiveness of any access control system will depend on an appropriate response by a person. Ideally, this person will be a trained Security Officer or Police Officer.

Level 0: No access control whatsoever.

Level 1: Signage Only. For example, where signs in a corridor indicate: "Staff Only: Do Not Enter" or "Restricted Access: Authorized Personnel Only." Proper signage provides security with the legal authority to challenge any person found within the designated area.

Level 2: Locked Door. They deter random entry and, depending on the door frame/door composition, lock type, and key control, delay unauthorized entry. However, every locked door can be compromised eventually.

Level 3: People. Receptionists and Security Officers (armed/unarmed) ranging from a single Security Officer standing at a corridor entrance to a large, multi-staffed gatehouse controlling access to a large plant or facility.

Level 4: Card Access/CCTV System. This system creates an audit trail. It can quickly restrict unauthorized entry, providing an effective card audit system is in place and lost/stolen cards are immediately updated and ruled out of the system.

Level 5: Biological Access Control Systems. These systems incorporate retinal scans, fingerprint scanning, photo image recognition, and voice analysis. This is a very expensive and elaborate system to maintain.

Level 6: Mantrap. The two-door system is an example, where only one person is allowed access at a time. The outer door must be closed before the inner door is opened. Most central stations have this feature.

Access Control Procedures

Every access control point must have clearly documented policies and procedures that tell the person there exactly what they are required to do. Authorized access lists must be up to date and an audit process must be in place to ensure all persons at that point have read and understood all required documents (i.e., sign-when-read sheet for post orders).

Security's Overall Responsibility for Access Control

The responsibility for access control doesn't end at the access point. It is every employee's responsibility to report suspicious persons, intruders, etc. to a responsible person.

If all persons beyond a certain point are required to display badges, security should clearly indicate so with a sign. Persons without badges should be challenged by anyone who encounters them (not just security!), or at the very least, be reported to security.

Too often Security Officers don't enforce access control policies out of a sense of "helpfulness." They want to demonstrate good public relations by trying to accommodate everyone. However, Security Officers must enforce access control policies.

Scenario

At a large corporate building, an individual demands access to one of the upper floors. Security denies access because the person does not have the appropriate authorization or identification. The person leaves the security desk, goes over to a bank of elevators out of security's view, pours an accelerant in the elevator and sets it on fire. Damage is minimal and is confined to the lobby area. What can we learn from this scenario?

Closed-Circuit Television Cameras

Many buildings have an elaborate Closed-Circuit Television Camera system (CCTV) that can be monitored directly on-site or off-site via a central station's remote CCTV monitoring capability. In most applications with a number of CCTV cameras, there is also a VCR capability and tapes are normally kept for a one- to two-week period. It is generally security's responsibility to ensure proper tape rotation.

At some sites, someone can be literally tracked around the property via CCTV. At others, cameras are only installed at critical access or egress points. There is also the capability of having the CCTV system only activate and start taping when an intrusion alarm is activated. Periodically, the tapes may need to be reviewed to examine a specific incident. Most tapes have a variable speed replay that allows you to play back at a faster-than-normal rate until you see the incident you are looking for. For very serious incidents, however, tapes are often reviewed in "real time" to ensure nothing is missed.

Monitoring of CCTV systems can be a tedious business. The task is often made easier by a multiplex style system whereby one monitor is trained on a critical area while others jump through a sequence of camera locations. You can, in effect, conduct a visual patrol of your property. The eye is generally sensitive to motion so you usually detect someone moving when they are on camera. However, if someone is just standing there, it can take a few moments before you register his or her presence.

Placement of CCTV cameras is of great importance when developing a viable system of countermeasures. It is generally advisable for property owners to seek the advice of a security consultant to determine the most cost effective CCTV system. Whatever system is chosen, it must be integrated with all of the other existing countermeasures.

REVIEW QUESTIONS

Level A

1. Define the 4D approach to access control.
2. What are the three components of effective countermeasures?
3. State what a vulnerability analysis is and indicate where it could be used.

Level B

1. Give five examples for each countermeasure: people, hardware, and software.

2. How can a CCTV system act as a countermeasure within a building's access control system?

3. Restate the access control continuum as a series of enclosed circles. Some refer to this model as the "onion-skin theory of access control." Which access control continuum model do you prefer? Why?

Level C

1. You are covering an access control desk. It is 2:00 p.m. on a Sunday. Your post orders clearly state all persons seeking access to the 14th floor executive area must show positive company identification and be on an authorized list. A man in a jogging outfit approaches you at the desk and gives you a business card indicating he is Jack Smith, VP of finance (the card is a bit smudged and crinkled). The name *Jack Smith* is on your access list, but you don't know him and he does not have any positive identification on him. He states he *must* get into his office to obtain material for an important stakeholders meeting on Monday. What would you do and say? (He is starting to become very belligerent.)

ASSISTING EMOTIONALLY DISTURBED PERSONS

LEARNING OUTCOMES

At the conclusion of this chapter, you will be able to

- Identify effective strategies for dealing with emotionally disturbed persons
- Understand some of the dos and don'ts for dealing with emotionally disturbed persons

OFFICER SAFETY CONSIDERATIONS

At some point in your security career, you will be called upon to assist an emotionally disturbed person. Your best preparation is to take a crisis intervention course or seminar to help you develop effective coping strategies.

A very small proportion of emotionally disturbed persons are a danger to others. Nonetheless, when dealing with them, your safety, the safety of your colleagues, and the safety of those around you are paramount. When an emotionally disturbed person is in crisis, it is critical that you immediately request police assistance if you feel your safety, the safety of the person, or the safety of anyone in the area is in jeopardy. Disengage and monitor the situation until the arrival of police. What follows are some brief suggestions on what you can do to successfully assist emotionally disturbed persons.

Strategies for Dealing with Emotionally Disturbed Persons

You may encounter an emotionally disturbed person who is in short-term or long-term crisis. A short-term crisis might be due to the ingestion of drugs or narcotics; a long-term crisis might be due to the loss of a job, suicidal tendencies, a chronic medical problem, or psychological problem. Unless specifically trained, you are not going to be able to diagnose what has triggered the crisis or what the specifics of the person's malady are.

Focus on the *behaviour* of the person. Behavioural cues will range from unresponsive lack of awareness to hyperactive, loud yelling, and erratic behaviour. Prior to intervening, ask yourself: Will I be able to improve the situation? If the person is not causing a disturbance, does not require obvious medical attention, and is not a threat to him- or herself or anyone else, is it necessary to intervene? Could I effectively deal with the situation by monitoring the person until he or she leaves? After all, it is not a crime to be an emotionally disturbed person. Remember, it is the behaviour of individuals that must determine your response.

Your best weapon is *empathy*. Above all, don't patronize the person. Table 18.1 identifies some dos and don'ts for dealing with emotionally disturbed persons.

TABLE 18.1 Dos and Don'ts for Dealing with Emotionally Disturbed Persons	
Do	**Rationale**
Speak to the person in a normal voice showing them the same respect you would anyone else.	Even though he or she might not respond verbally, your tone of voice will have a positive effect on him or her. Always consider the possibility that the person may be deaf.
Be aware of your positioning and maintain Condition Yellow.	Some persons with serious mental health problems are known to carry weapons (usually edged weapons) and will use them if provoked or if they feel threatened or cornered.
Attempt to have the person relocate out of a crowded area, but not so that you are isolated.	Adverse crowd reaction can provoke an emotionally disturbed person into displaying aggressive behaviour.
Visually check the person for any sign of a medical condition (e.g., Medic Alert bracelet).	Many persons suffering medical conditions have been mistakenly thought to be emotionally disturbed when what they really needed was immediate medical attention.
Activate the emergency medical system and treat as a medical emergency if you feel the person requires immediate medical attention.	Exercise standard precautions that you normally would in applying first aid.
Attempt to be on the same level as the person. If the person is sitting at a table, and it is safe to do so, sit down opposite him or her maintaining an appropriate reactionary gap.	Being at the same level makes you appear less threatening.
Try to get the person to agree to a simple request. If he or she is standing in front of a door say, "Let's move off to the side so we don't block people."	If the person agrees to the simple request, chances are he or she will agree to an important request (e.g., leave the area).
Ask other people in the area if they know the person.	The person might be a regular and someone may know a friend or relative who can be called to assist.

Call for backup (if available) to act as cover person.

The call ensures additional help is available if the situation deteriorates.

Try to find out as much information about the person as possible. Name, age, address, tattoos, physical deformities, clothing, and objects they have.

This information will be invaluable the next time you, or someone else, has to deal with this person. Fully document the occurrence.

Don't	Rationale
Patronize the person (e.g., "Yah, I hear those voices all the time too").	The person may be emotionally disturbed, but he or she is not stupid. He or she will know when you are making fun of him or her.
Yell or berate the person.	Any sympathy you may have had with bystanders will be quickly lost.
Arbitrarily take away the person's possessions.	It might just be a dirty shopping bag to you, but to the person it might be his or her life's possessions.
Automatically assume the person is dangerous.	Persons with mental illness have an emotional empathy and awareness that many of us lack. Often, they will respond to you in the same way you are treating them.
Automatically assume the person is harmless.	Many drugs and narcotics can generate rapid mood swings in a person, making him or her meek and submissive one moment and homicidal the next.
Judge on the basis of appearance.	Behaviour must dictate your response.
Expect pressure-point tactics to always work.	The person's nerves may be deadened so he or she doesn't feel pain.
Be surprised if when you attempt a simple escort, the person reacts as if you had hit him or her.	Some drugs/medical conditions may heighten nerve sensitivity.

Scenario

It is 10:00 a.m. on a weekday. You are the only Security Officer working in a medium-sized mall and are just coming out of the corridor from your security office. All of a sudden, you hear a blood-curdling yell coming from the food court area. You briskly walk out to the food court and several of the patrons sitting at tables all point to a male standing at one of the food counters. He looks very disheveled, has long black hair, and a very pale complexion. The girl behind the counter appears very frightened. You ask her if she is okay and she says, "Yes. He just came here and yelled." As you begin to approach the male from the #3 position, he lets out another scream and turns to face you. His eyes are saucer size and his face is ashen. His right eye is blackened and there are numerous cuts and bruises on his face and neck area. You have visually checked the area and there are no other persons nearby, although a number of people are sitting at their tables watching you and him. His hands are out of his pockets and he is just standing there, looking at you.

You are trained in defensive tactics (including edged-weapon defence), are wearing body armour, and are carrying handcuffs and a side-handled baton. You have witnessed the male causing a disturbance and could lawfully arrest him, or direct him to leave the property. Based on his size, demeanour, and proximity you are confident you can control him physically if required.

You initiate conversation:

Security: How are you today?

Male: They are here.

Security: Did you buy anything here? Is that your pop? (You already know the answer but you want the person to focus on you.)

Male: They didn't get me.

Security: Let's go back to the security office, okay?

(A tactical decision was made not to arrest the suspect. The suspect voluntarily accompanies security to the security office. Once in the security office, the Security Officer sits behind the desk, leaves the door open, and has the person sit in front of the desk. The person has direct access to the door. Remember: the person is not under arrest at this point. He voluntarily came back to the office.)

Security: Are you okay? What happened to your face?

Male: I like to test people.

Security: Did that happen here?

Male: No.

Security: My name is Doug. What is your first name?

Male: John.

Security: Thanks. Do you have any identification on you? I have to put in a report about my speaking with you.

(The subject produces positive ID verifying his name, address, and date of birth.)

Security: Thank you. Is anyone looking for you right now?

Male: Not now.

Security: Do you mind if I just check with the police? I want to make sure everything is okay.

Male: (No response)

(Police are contacted and are told the subject is not under arrest but has attended on consent. A car is not necessary at this time, but you just want to verify with them that they were not looking for a missing person. Note: Some police radio dispatchers will assist this way if they have dealt with you before. Others insist on sending a car. It is at the discretion of the dispatcher. Police advise that the subject is known to them but is not wanted or reported missing at this time.)

> Security: I'm going to have to ask you not to come back to the mall because of your yelling. You can't yell like that in the mall. You scare a lot of people.

> Male: Yeah. I know.

(The suspect is issued a six-month bar notice. On consent, a Polaroid photograph is taken of the suspect to assist other security in identifying him. Taking photographs of barred subjects will depend on your company and site's policy. A full report is completed.)

Total elapsed time: 15 minutes.

If the subject had been arrested, Security would have been out of the mall for at least one hour. If the subject had just been asked to leave, identification would not have been made, nor would the photograph have been taken.

REVIEW QUESTIONS

Level C

1. You are on break relief for the person at the access control desk in a large multi-use complex where commercial and residential tenants reside. It is 3:00 a.m. in the middle of January and a cold weather alert has been posted. You observe a street person sleeping outside in the revolving door alcove. The doors are secure and won't be opened until 7:00 a.m. Your post orders specifically state, "No vagrants are allowed to sleep on the property," due to past tenant and resident complaints. What would you do? (In your answer, try to incorporate everything you have learned so far in this textbook.)

2. Complete a threat assessment matrix for all the areas described in the Scenario in this chapter. Your matrix must include three columns with headings: Problem Area, Area of Responsibility, and Focus Points.

CRIME PREVENTION

LEARNING OUTCOMES

At the conclusion of this chapter, you will be able to

- Demonstrate an understanding of the history and definition of CPTED
- Define crime and crime prevention
- Identify the four approaches to crime prevention
- State and explain the CPTED premise
- Identify and explain the three CPTED strategies: natural access control, natural surveillance, and territorial reinforcement
- Identify CPTED concept relationships, strategy activities, and planning requirements
- Identify CPTED limitations

INTRODUCTION

Some may question why private Security Officers should learn about crime prevention. These people would have us believe crime prevention is solely the domain of public policing. In truth, to be effective, it is fundamental that any crime prevention strategy involve the community. Private security certainly must be considered as part of that community. Perhaps some of the reluctance to see private security as crime preventers stems from the concern that private security only focuses on the profit motive. This is a legitimate concern and must be addressed.

Throughout this textbook, we have emphasized the preventive nature of private security. Businesses have a much greater concern in preventing crime from happening in the first place, rather than having an excellent response mechanism. Based on The Theft Triangle (see Chapter 9), we learned that effective security countermeasures in the form of effective access control, alarm systems, security staff, and other target-hardening approaches can reduce the *opportunity* for a crime to occur. Such measures are doubly effective when the *desire* and the *motive* to commit the crime are also reduced through effective crime prevention strategies.

The police are not security consultants. For a number of reasons (one of the main ones being liability concerns), police Crime Prevention Officers will not provide a detailed report to clients recommending specific actions that can be taken to reduce opportunity, desire, and motive to commit crime. Their crime prevention strategies are focused on the larger community and, unless the level of crime at a particular property requires their focused attention, they deal with the broader community.

In many cases, those who are closest to the situation are also the ones best-suited to suggest a solution. This is true, providing they have the ability to truly understand the problem and are able to articulate what they see the solution to be. Who could be closer to the micro-community than Security Officers working in the local mall? If those Security Officers understand the rudiments of crime prevention, they can be of tremendous value to the client and the security company. In addition, they will be a valuable resource to the local Crime Prevention Officer. The best results are always achieved when both the police and private security work in tandem.

We will also review one of the most effective, and simplest, of the crime prevention strategies that can be easily learned and applied by private Security Officers: Crime Prevention Through Environmental Design (CPTED).

CRIME PREVENTION

Definition of Crime

Crime is "an act committed in violation of a law prohibiting it, an act omitted in violation of a law ordering it, or an offense against morality."[1] Note: This definition is distinct from "criminal offence."

Definition of Crime Prevention

Crime prevention is "...the anticipation, recognition and appraisal of a crime risk and initiation of action to remove or reduce it."[2]

TABLE 19.1 Four Approaches to Crime Prevention	
Approach	**Area**
1 Root cause	Social development
2 General opportunity reduction	Neighbourhood Watch, employee education
3 Specific opportunity reduction	Situational crime prevention (e.g., CPTED)
4 Systems or comprehensive approach	Multiple organizations involved in strategic planning and implementation

Source: Fennelly (1999: 4)

Canadian Crime Prevention Initiatives

Ideally, Canadian crime prevention should comprise

- Promotion of crime prevention and social development activities
- Reduction of fear of crime through public education
- Co-ordination of existing crime prevention activities (in particular those related to violent crimes and crimes against persons and property)
- Serve as a resource for those who want to be active in community safety activities[3]

Evaluation of Crime Prevention Methods

Crime prevention methods can be evaluated through their ability to

- Increase knowledge
- Change attitudes
- Alter actions
- Mobilize communities
- Reduce crime rates
- Enhance the quality of life[4]

Crime Prevention Principles

- Preventing crime is as important as arresting criminals.
- Preventing disorder is as important as preventing crime.
- Reducing both crime and disorder requires the co-operation of police, security, and all people within the neighbourhood.[5]

The Theft Triangle

We examined The Theft Triangle in Chapter 9, but it is worth reviewing in the context of crime prevention.

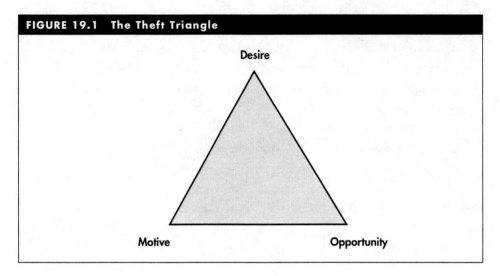

FIGURE 19.1 The Theft Triangle

Motive. The reason to steal (i.e., resentment for being passed over for promotion, being overburdened in debt, etc.)

Desire. It builds on motive by imagining satisfaction or gratification that would come from a potential act

Opportunity. The absence of barriers that prevent someone from stealing

Note: Fear of discovery is the most important deterrent to internal theft.

Key Components of Opportunity Reduction

1. Criminal behaviour is learned behaviour.
2. Reducing criminal opportunity reduces the opportunity to learn criminal behaviour.
3. Improved security measures and increased level of surveillance by the public can lessen criminal opportunity.
4. Criminal opportunities must be reduced on a national basis to achieve long-range crime prevention.
5. Police and security are in a pivotal position to reduce crime and should be trained in crime prevention and become involved in planning community activities where their services may be called for later.
6. Insurance, security hardware, security service providers, police, and all those involved in crime prevention must exchange information.[6]

CRIME PREVENTION THROUGH ENVIRONMENTAL DESIGN

What does CPTED stand for?

CPTED is the acronym for Crime Prevention Through Environmental Design. It is pronounced "Sep Ted."

Why should Security Officers know about CPTED?

- To increase chances of obtaining a full-time position in any organization
- To add value to any future employment position
- To add value to what you are contributing to your employer
- Self-development
- It demonstrates commitment to life-long learning
- To bring a fresh, new outlook and expand the frontiers of CPTED
- To contribute to the overall increase in the quality of life of your community

Employment Opportunities for Those Trained in CPTED

Police – Crime prevention specialist
Police – Community Police Officer
Police – Crime analyst
Security – Security consultant
Planning – Planner or architect
Insurance – Insurance adjuster
Law – Lawyer or legal assistant
Opportunities apply to a plethora of other occupations.

What You Need to Know about CPTED

1. What CPTED stands for.
2. Definitions of crime, crime prevention, The Theft Triangle, the CPTED premise, natural access control, natural surveillance, territorial reinforcement, 3D concept.
3. Four approaches to crime prevention.
4. Crime prevention principles.
5. Evaluation of crime prevention methods.
6. Six key components of opportunity reduction.
7. CPTED history: early forerunners and founders.
8. Application of CPTED strategies: natural access control, natural surveillance, territorial reinforcement.
9. Identify CPTED concept relationships.
10. Identify CPTED strategy activities.
11. Identify CPTED planning requirements.
12. Identify CPTED limitations.
13. Identify components of a CPTED report.
14. Classify statements as to their classification within the 3D model.

CPTED FUNDAMENTALS

Premise of CPTED

The CPTED premise is: "The proper *design* and effective *use* of the built environment can lead to a reduction in the incidence and fear of crime and to an increase in the quality of life."[7] Although this definition need not be memorized verbatim, the two key words: *design* and *use* must be remembered. *Environment* refers to the environment of the victim, not the environment of the criminal (i.e., CPTED focuses on situational factors, not criminal predisposition to commit crime). CPTED initially focuses on specific opportunity reduction. However, when CPTED is applied during the design phase of a property, the systems or comprehensive approach can be considered.

History of CPTED

Table 19.2 provides an overview of the history of CPTED.

TABLE 19.2	History of CPTED	
Year	**Event**	**Comment**
1961	Sociologist Jane Jacobs publishes The Death and Life of Great American Cities.	The book is critical of post-war policies that catered to the needs of automobiles at the expense of local community life. Traffic routes and segregation of land use into large shopping malls, industrial parks, and entertainment complexes had removed pedestrian traffic from the street and had destroyed opportunities for everyday social interaction.
1971	C. Ray Jeffery publishes Crime Prevention Through Environmental Design.	Jeffery coins the term "CPTED."
1972	Architect Oscar Newman publishes Defensible Space.	Influenced by Jane Jacobs, Newman compiles research and makes observations in St. Louis and New York. He identifies numerous features of public housing design that would reduce crime.
Late 1970s	Interest in CPTED declines in the United States.	Newman's ideas are dismissed as "environmentalist determinism."
		He is accused of "oversimplification" and neglecting social causes such as poverty, unemployment, and racism.
1980	Dept. of Justice publishes a review concerning the link between crime and the built environment.	The review concludes that relationship between physical environment and crime is weaker than had been claimed by Newman. There is an overall rise in conservatism through the U.S. The favoured punitive response to crime leads to a loss of federal support of CPTED.

1970s and 1980s	CPTED theories are applied successfully throughout Europe.	There are a large number of public housing projects.
1991	Timothy Crowe publishes Crime Prevention Through Environmental Design, First Edition.	The book is accepted as the standard industry reference on CPTED.
1990s	There is a resurgence of interest in CPTED.	Many courses are offered by the National Crime Prevention Institute and through local police services.
2000	Timothy Crowe publishes Crime Prevention Through Environmental Design, Second Edition.	The book is long awaited by many in the security industry. It is still considered as the standard industry reference on CPTED.

Source: Sorensen (1998: 2–5)

Validation of CPTED

Criminology theories support the principles of CPTED.

Broken Window Theory. "Small signs of neighbourhood decay can result in a downward spiral of steadily worsening crime." (Wilson & Kelling, 1982.)

Hot Spot Analysis. "Criminals choose to commit crime and that they weigh the likely costs and benefits of committing particular criminal actions in particular areas." A *hot spot* refers to places where crime is highly concentrated.

Rational Choice Theory. "Sees crime as within the offender's control and does not believe that social and psychological factors predispose the individual to criminality." (Cornish et al., 1986.)[8]

CPTED STRATEGIES

Natural Access Control

- A design concept directed at decreasing crime opportunity.
- The space should give natural indication of when people are allowed and not allowed access.
- It can be organized (Security Officers), mechanical (locks), or natural (river or swamp).[9]

Natural Surveillance

- A design concept directed primarily at keeping an intruder under observation.
- It may keep an intruder out because of an increased perception of risk.
- It can be organized (security patrol, police patrol), mechanical (lighting or CCTV), or natural (window).
- Traditionally, design concepts of access control and surveillance placed emphasis on mechanical or organized crime prevention techniques.

- Recent approaches to the physical design of environment have shifted to the use of natural opportunities for crime prevention opportunities provided by the environment.
- This shift has led to the concept of "territoriality."[10]

Territorial Reinforcement

- Physical design can contribute to a sense of territorial influence.
- It includes natural surveillance and access control principles.
- It was first noted in public housing environment.
- It brings the balance needed between design for crime prevention and design for effective use of the environment.
- A natural strategy incorporates existing behaviour patterns and reinforces positive behaviour.

CPTED Concept Relationship

Author Timothy Crowe summarizes the CPTED design concepts in Figure 19.2 and Figure 19.3.

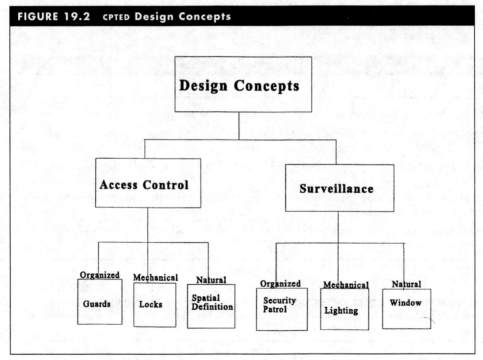

FIGURE 19.2 CPTED **Design Concepts**

Source: Crowe (2000: 37–38)

FIGURE 19.3   Primary and Secondary CPTED **Design Concepts**

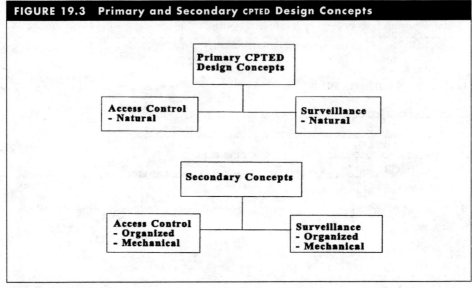

Source: Crowe (2000: 37–38)

Note: The shift from organized and mechanical concepts to natural concepts leads to the success of territorial reinforcement.

TABLE 19.3   CPTED Strategy Activities

Activity	Example
1 Place safe activity in an unsafe location.	Plant a community garden in a vacant lot.
2 Place an unsafe activity in a safe location to overcome the vulnerability of those activities.	Place a night bank deposit area in a public waiting area.
3 Provide clear border definition of controlled space.	Place a wooden ornamental fence around your lawn.
4 Redesign the use of space to provide natural barriers to conflicting activities.	In a park, place basketball hoops on the other side of a hill where seniors' benches are.
5 Redesign space to increase the perception and reality of natural surveillance.	Relocate library study carrels closer to the stacks.

Source: Crowe (2000: 40–41)

TABLE 19.4   CPTED Planning Requirements

Type	Comment
1 Crime analysis	This is available from police and/or security reports.
2 Demographics	They describe the nature of the population of a given city, district, or neighbourhood. They are available from city managers, city planning department, or mayor's department.
3 Land use	This describes and depicts allocation and use of land.

4 Observations	Visit the space at different days/times. Observations include pedestrian vehicle counts, and maintenance of yards and fences. Gauge the reaction of residents to your presence.
5 Resident or user interviews	They are required to balance other data sources.
	Gauge people's perceptions of where they feel safe.

Source: Crowe (2000: 41–43)

SPACE DEFINITIONS

Defining Space

CPTED "actors" include:

Normal Users. Persons whom you desire in a certain space.

Abnormal Users. Persons whom you do not desire to be in a certain place.

Observers. Those persons who have to be in that space to support the "human function." (e.g., someone sitting out on their front porch watching the street).[11]

Successful CPTED strategies are required to be

- Understandable
- Practical for normal users of the space (they know more about what is going on and their own well-being depends on their environment operating properly).

Crowe suggests three fundamental concepts apply to the dimensions of human space:

1. All human space has some *designated* purpose.
2. All human space has social, cultural, legal, or physical *definitions* that prescribe the desired and acceptable behaviours.
3. All human space is *designed* to support and control the desired behaviours.[12]

The 3D Concept

The 3D concept provides a guide to determine how space is designed and used.[13] The 3D concept is fundamental to the application of the CPTED strategy. It encompasses:

- Designation
- Definition
- Design

Designation

- What is the designated purpose of this space?
- What was it originally intended to be used for?
- How well does the space support its current use? Its intended use?
- Is there conflict?

Definition

- How is the space defined?
- Is it clear who owns it?
- Where are its borders?
- Are there social or cultural definitions that affect how that space is used?
- Are the legal or administrative rules clearly set out and reinforced in policy?
- Are there signs?
- Is there conflict or confusion between the designated purpose and definition?

Design

- How well does the physical design support the intended function?
- How well does the physical design support the definition of the desired or accepted behaviours?
- Does the physical design conflict with or impede the productive use of the space or the proper functioning of the intended human activity?
- Is there confusion or conflict in the manner in which the physical design is intended to control behaviour?

Sample Test Question

The question, "Is there confusion or conflict in the manner in which the physical design is intended to control behaviour?" is an example of:

a)   Designation

b)   Definition

c)   Design

d)   All of the above

e)   None of the above

Answer: c

CPTED LIMITATIONS

Standards

There is no prescribed format that must be followed when applying the CPTED approach. Some individuals have incorrectly applied the CPTED approach to areas that are too large for specific CPTED strategies to affect.

CPTED: **Art or Science?**

Traditionally, CPTED has been more of an art than a science. Significant quantitative assessment of its effectiveness is only now being tracked in a large enough sample to provide for strategic analysis.

Training

There are no CPTED training standards. However, CPTED training is available.

- CPTED Level 1 and 2 Practitioner certification is offered through the National Crime Prevention Institute, Louisville, Kentucky
- Several community colleges in Ontario offer CPTED Level 1 (Durham College, Conestoga College)
- Many police services in Ontario now provide CPTED training to their own members and, increasingly, such training is also being offered to the public (Ottawa-Carleton, London Police Service, Peel Regional Police)
- Many in the CPTED community are pushing for a standardized approach to CPTED training
- At this time, anyone can call themselves a CPTED consultant
- Existing associations (International CPTED Association) and newly formed associations (Ontario CPTED Association) are addressing the issue of CPTED training

THE CPTED REPORT

Spatial Data Management Style

As with any type of consulting work, once a CPTED review has been completed, the observations and recommendations need to be presented to the client in a report format. Crowe advocates a spatial data management style report that uses a matrix-style report broken down into three columns (Possible Solutions, Advantages, and Disadvantages). With a slight modification in reporting style (using General Comments instead of Disadvantages) as suggested by Mike Fenton, Director of Consulting and Sales Support, Intercon Security, I have used this type of report for CPTED consulting assignments and have noted that, in general, it reduces the overall report length by almost 50 per cent of what a standard, narrative report would be.

It is often beneficial to include photographs in the CPTED report to demonstrate to the client the specifics of what is being discussed. See Appendix A for a sample of the first three pages of a CPTED report. This report was prepared using the spatial data management style.

CPTED **Report Training**

Surprisingly, it does not take very long to learn the fundamentals of writing a CPTED report. Providing you have "done your homework" during the CPTED review and have asked all of the right questions, the actual report is much easier to complete than the traditional narrative style report. Part of the reason may be that CPTED is based on a common sense approach that naturally leads to a spatial data management style report.

THE FUTURE

CPTED and Private Security

There are definitely career opportunities within private security for trained CPTED practitioners. CPTED principles can be easily learned and applied by the front-line Security Officer. Those who are trained in CPTED principles can certainly add value to their employer.

CPTED and Policing

Many police services (e.g., Peel Regional Police, London Police Service, York Regional Police, Ottawa-Carleton Police, and Toronto Police Service) have incorporated CPTED into the services provided by their Crime Prevention Officers. Police services now actively work with architects and planners to ensure fundamental CPTED strategies are considered at the design stage of new buildings.

CPTED ASSOCIATIONS AND FURTHER INFORMATION

There is a plethora of literature, associations, and Internet sites on CPTED. Indeed, if you go on the Internet and type in "CPTED" you will be provided with an abundance of related sites. I have summarized some of the ones that I am personally familiar with.

The CPTED Institute
c/o The Mississauga Crime Prevention Association
110 Dundas Street West
Mississauga, Ontario L5B 1H3
Tel: (905) 803-8118
Fax: (905) 803-8841

The Mississauga CPTED Advisory Committee
City of Mississauga
Planning and Building Department
11th Floor
300 City Centre Drive
Mississauga, Ontario L5B 3C1
Tel: (905) 896-5522
Fax: (905) 896-5553
Web site: **www.city.mississauga.on.ca**

International CPTED Association (ICA)
International Headquarters
439 Queen Alexandra Way SE
Calgary, Alberta T2J 3P2
Tel: (403) 225-3595
Fax: (403) 278-4965
Web site: **www.cpted.net**

Table 19.5 provides a number of CPTED-related Internet sites.

TABLE 19.5 CPTED Internet Sites	
Web Site	**Description**
security.macarthur.uws.edu.au/links.htm	A complete listing of all Web sites relating to situational crime prevention and security issues, categorized by country
securitymanagement.com/library/000199.html	A complete article by Mary S. Smith titled "Crime Prevention Through Environmental Design in Parking Facilities"
peelpolice.on.ca/council.html	CPTED case study on Council Ring Plaza
www.sgc.gc.ca	A police reference manual on crime prevention and diversion with youth (the entire 132-page text can be downloaded)
www.replacefear.com	Canadian Crime Prevention Centre
www.crime-prevention.org/ncpc/	National Crime Prevention Council
canada.justice.gc.ca	Department of Justice Canada
www.nps.ca	Public access to CPIC regarding stolen vehicles, licences, etc.

REVIEW QUESTIONS

Level A

1. Distinguish between "desire" and "opportunity" as they relate to The Theft Triangle.
2. State the CPTED premise.
3. Who originally coined the term "CPTED"?
4. State five CPTED planning requirements.
5. What is the 3D concept?

Level B

1. By planting a flower garden outside the front of your home, what CPTED strategy are you employing if your intent is to stop your neighbour from walking across your front lawn with his dog?
2. Some would suggest that the phrase "place a safe activity in an unsafe location" should be reworded because it may increase liability exposure (i.e., should we be causing an activity to take place in an "unsafe location"?). How could you reword that CPTED strategy?
3. Why is it appropriate to refer to CPTED as a "situational crime prevention method"?

Level C

1. Research the Internet to obtain CPTED information relating to
   - Public housing
   - Parking garages
   - Hospitals
   - Schools

CONCLUSION

A lot of material has been covered in this textbook. You should now understand the importance of the various types of security patrols in providing the level of protection required by clients. My only hope is that Security Officers who read this material are able to successfully apply it to their normal patrol duties. If the officer safety principles presented in this textbook assist even one Security Officer in avoiding serious injury or death, I consider writing this textbook a worthwhile endeavour.

I am very encouraged by the spirit of co-operation and willingness to form partnerships with private security (and all community stakeholders) that many police services are now showing. Organizations such as the Ontario Association of Chiefs of Police, and community crime prevention councils and committees provide opportunities for idea sharing among members of the policing community, citizens' groups, and private business.

As someone who has been part of both the policing and private security community, I hope this spirit of co-operation and partnership continues. The bridge between the private security and police communities is in place. All we need to do is ensure that adequate supports remain in place to support the increasing load that both groups must bear.

Certain aspects of security patrols I did not address in this textbook include:

- Bicycle patrols
- Vehicle patrols
- Patrolling with canines
- Patrolling with horses (some security agencies now have horse patrols)

- Arrest procedures
- Criminal code
- Defensive tactics considerations

Some of these are covered in other texts and courses offered by community colleges and universities. In addition, throughout this text I have supplied a number of reference contacts that will help readers obtain further information. As well, the Bibliography provides excellent material for further reference. The Internet is also an excellent source of information relating to all aspects of security and crime prevention.

I am very interested in feedback on this textbook and can be contacted through the publisher.

Good luck in your security career.

APPENDIX A:

CPTED Security Review of Anyplace Garage, Anytown

Purpose: To reduce the potential for criminal activity, increase usage by normal users, and improve normal user comfort level

Prepared by: Doug Henrich, et al.

Possible Solutions	Advantages	General Comments
Overview	low.	
General		
This garage presents some security challenges including:		
Low-pressure sodium lighting		
Lack of "way-finding" signage		
Lack of clearly defined "transition zones" between vehicular and pedestrian traffic		
Lack of visibility for existing active security devices (i.e., crisis alarms and CCTV cameras)		
Positive factors include:		
Segregation of motorcycle parking		
Good celebration and transition through ramp usage at Alpha Street entrance		
Well lit elevators and stairwells		
Extensive CCTV monitoring		
Absence of graffiti		
Light fixtures located over the vehicles instead of over roadways		
Elevators that open into security vestibules		
Clean and garbage-free garage area		
Our recommendations fol-		

Possible Solutions	Advantages	General Comments
Entrance		
Both Entrances		
Illuminate entrance sign for night usage.	Reduces confusion for night visitors	Low cost
		High priority
Place parking location signs in immediate and neighbouring vicinity to identify parking facility (subject to municipal approval).	Potentially increases facility usage	
Beta Street Entrance		
Change sidewalk tiling near Beta St. S/E stairs to a pattern different from public sidewalk.	Improves transition zone from public to semi-public space	Low cost
		High priority
Change colour, or extend awning further outwards over parking entrance to differentiate from neighbouring awnings.	Celebrates garage entrance	
Place "Parking" sign above awning.	Reduces normal user confusion	
Signage		
Numbering	Improves reporting of crime	Low cost
Number all parking spots with 12-in. (30 cm) or larger numbers or separate each level into quadrants and provide unique identifiers (i.e., Red Zone, Blue Zone)	Improves statistical analysis of theft and vandalism reports	High priority
	Improves security response to problems in the garage	Note: Approximately 40% of numbers should be on walls and pillars. The balance of the numbers can be applied to the floor in front of parking spots. "Reserved" spots should be reserved only by number and signage stating Reserved, and not by company name, employee name, or initials).
	Standard garage performance feature to assist patrons in finding their car	
	Helps reduce/eliminate false car theft reports	
Warning Signage	Security through education	Low cost
Signs using the typical parking lot Entrance/Exit signage wording should be erected on all stairwell doors and at two other locations for every half floor area. An alternative is signage stating "Suspicious??? Call Security/ Police at: ###-####." This wording may be preferable if management believes that the longer wording may convey a siege mentality or disturb normal users.	Possible prevention of some attacks	High priority
	Display of the security phone number is a proven deterrent	With respect to displaying the security phone number, our experience is that most persons will not walk back into the building to report a crime in progress. If the number is available, many people who have cellular phones will call to report a crime in progress.
	Permanent security solution	
	Improves normal user comfort level	
	Enhances reporting of crime	

APPENDIX B:
Security Report Analysis

FORMULATION OF PROBLEM STATEMENT

Interpretation of crime patterns requires consideration of the following elements. Note: We will focus on theft of cash/property.

Target/Victim Characteristics

The open concept and large floor area of Location #1 provides ample opportunity for a culprit (or culprits) to gain ready access to a victim's change purse/petty cash stored in unlocked drawers/filing cabinets or on desks in open areas. As well, this open concept facilitates the removal of laptop computers left unattended on top of desks or in offices. In addition, the culprit would appear to have prior knowledge as to when new electronic merchandise is delivered and who is unable to secure his or her desk drawers/filing cabinets. This knowledge extends to thefts that occur on all floors. It is likely that the culprit knows each of the victims, their work habits, and where they store valuables.

Offender Characteristics

Pattern analysis suggests that the culprit must work, or have worked, in the building. In addition, the culprit must work in a capacity that allows for multi-floor, after-hours access. As well, the culprit may have access to building keys as some of the targets have been inside locked premises. The culprit would also have access to a ready means of disposing of the laptop computers (i.e., friends, associates, relatives). Theft patterns may also match spending requirements of the culprit (i.e., rent, mortgage, car payments). There is also a likelihood the theft patterns will be opposite to the times when the culprit would normally be paid.

Time of the Offence

Some caution must be exercised in interpreting the time that the offences took place as the reports show that time estimates are only approximate. This has been addressed by using a probability matrix format that brackets the time span of each of the reported offences. Analysis of Figure B.1, Theft Comparison by Day of Week, and Figure B.2, Theft Comparison by Month, suggests that Thursdays from 17:00 to 21:00 and the weekends were the most frequent periods targeted for theft of cash and property. As well, April, June, and November appear to be the months with the highest frequency of theft occurrences. It is also significant that during the months of May, August, and October, no thefts of property or cash were reported. The cyclical pattern established here should be cross-referenced with vacation schedules of those who work in the building and possible suspects.

Modus Operandi

The methodology of the cash and property thefts appear similar. It is likely the same person or persons are responsible for both types of theft. Vehicular break-ins may be of a random nature, however, and are not necessarily linked to the theft of cash/property. Cash thefts started in March 2000 and continued through to November 2000. They most likely stopped in November because people were no longer leaving cash accessible. The culprit then switched to laptop computers as his or her confidence had been boosted by previous success in the theft of cash. It is significant that on two occasions the culprit did not take all the cash. In one case, he or she took $30 of $40, and in another he or she took $100 of $200. A culprit from outside the building would not normally make that distinction. In many cases, when employees steal cash from the place they work in, they do not take all the money available. Perhaps they believe the theft will not be immediately detected if all the money is not taken and, thus, suspicion will not fall on the shift they worked when the theft occurred.

Spatial Aspects

Criminal acts are not randomly distributed geographically. The culprit must determine a means of access, a means of target identification, alternate escape routes, and a means of egress. Floor plans would be required to pinpoint the exact locations of the thefts in relation to each other and in relation to points of access/egress and natural surveillance. This is a point where follow-up is recommended.

Opportunity Factors

It appears existing security is a low-level deterrent to such thefts (as evidenced by the ease with which a terminated employee gained access to the building). This problem is compounded by the fact that many workers in the building are temporary and do not have keys to their desks, filing cabinets, and drawers, etc. It appears the culprit was aware of this fact and knew the specific individuals who lacked such keys.

System Response

Management must decide whether the priority is prevention of further thefts or apprehension of the culprit. Prevention should be possible through a combination of target hardening and the adoption of Crime Prevention Through Environmental Design (CPTED) principles.

There are a number of different strategies to apprehending culprits:

Statement Analysis. Possible suspects can be requested to provide handwritten statements detailing any knowledge, suggestions, or concerns they may have regarding the theft occurrences. (This can be done innocuously in the form of a survey that, in itself, should generate good will on the part of those not party to the thefts.) Properly executed statement analysis of such responses has an 80 per cent to 90 per cent likelihood of identifying possible suspects.

Sting Operation. A covert sting operation can be set up once possible suspects have been identified. This identification is necessary to make the sting operation more cost-effective.

Covert Surveillance. Covert surveillance using hidden cameras is also an option, but it is also potentially the most costly.

Follow-up

Once a suspect has been positively identified, police should be involved because they may have grounds to obtain a warrant to search the suspect's residence and possibly recover stolen property.

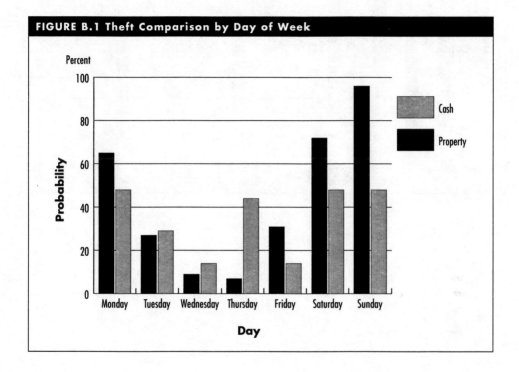

FIGURE B.1 Theft Comparison by Day of Week

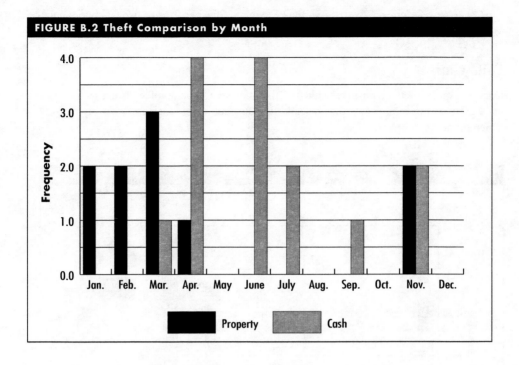

FIGURE B.2 Theft Comparison by Month

GLOSSARY

Abnormal users. Persons whose presence is not desired in a certain space.

Annunciator. An electrical device that indicates where a signal is originating from.

Brisance. The shattering power of an explosion.

Cascade system. A notification process where all persons are assigned specific persons to contact, who are, in turn, assigned specific persons to contact, and so on. This can be used to implement response to a bomb threat.

Central station. A central location which is established to monitor large numbers of alarms on a regular basis.

Combination patrol. Where the stairwell patrol is combined with the floor-by-floor patrol.

Complete patrol. Where a single stairwell is patrolled from top to bottom.

Condition Black. Blind panic.

Condition Orange. A state of alarm.

Condition Red. What looks wrong, is wrong. The focus is now on the threat. The Security Officer acts to control it using whatever degree of force is required. All systems are go.

Condition White. Environmental unawareness—this is the blissful state of most un-trained security personnel.

Condition Yellow. Relaxed, but alert and cautious, and not tense. Constant 360-degree surveillance of people, places, things, and actions. This should be the continuous state of all on-duty Security Officers, especially when they are on patrol.

Contact Officer. Is the primary investigator who initiates and conducts all the business of the contact. The Contact Officer is responsible for the chain of custody of any evidence.

Contract security. Security staff employed by a private security agency who provide se-curity services to other organizations on a contractual basis.

Countermeasure. Any activity that is implemented to reduce the risk of injury to persons and/or loss or damage to property.

Cover Officer. The officer who protects the Contact Officer by establishing a "force presence." This person devotes all attention to the action of the suspects and maintains a position of surveillance and control.

CPTED. Crime Prevention Through Environmental Design.

CPTED premise. The proper design and effective use of the built environment can lead to a reduction in the incidence and fear of crime and to an increase in the quality of life.

Crime. An act committed in violation of a law prohibiting it, an act omitted in violation of a law ordering it, or an offence against morality.

Crime prevention. The anticipation, recognition, and appraisal of a crime risk and initiation of action to remove and reduce it.

Crime scene. Any situation that has arisen from the commission of a serious criminal offence and includes physical evidence relating to the offence.

Criticality. The impact the occurrence of an event may have on an entity, business, or individual.

Crossover floors. Stairwell doors are not locked on these floors, or they are released during a fire alarm to allow access to other stairwells as an alternate escape route.

Crowd. A group of individuals assembled together for a common, lawful purpose.

Dead zone. An area where a hand-held radio will not transmit and/or receive communications.

Desire. It builds on the motive by imagining satisfaction or gratification that would come from a potential act.

Disengagement. Always an option in any situation.

Dry systems. Pressurized air is in the sprinkler pipe at the sprinkler head. For there to be a sprinkler discharge, water has to flow to the head first. Dry systems are primarily used in underground garages where the temperature may go below freezing.

Early closing patrol. A security patrol to observe and report on merchants who have closed prior to the time prescribed within their lease.

Emergency. Any condition that requires immediate action and, if left unchecked, that would cause injury or death to any person or damage property.

Emotionally disturbed person. You may encounter an emotionally disturbed person who is in short-term or long-term crisis. The crisis may be short term (i.e., due to ingestion of drugs or narcotics) or long term (due to loss of a job, suicidal tendencies, a chronic medical problem, or psychological problem).

Empty-handed techniques.

    Soft: pressure point control tactics

    Hard: strikes or blows

Galvanometer. Detects changes in electric potential from an intruder.

Gang. A group of individuals joined together with a common criminal intent.

Group. A collection of like-minded individuals joined together with a common purpose.

Hot spot. A place where crime is highly concentrated.

In-house security. Security staff employed directly by the company it provides security services for.

Intermediate weapons. Baton, pepper spray.

Late-opening patrol. A security patrol to observe and report on merchants that have not opened for business at the time prescribed within their lease.

Lease-line violation. It occurs when a merchant extends its displays beyond the lease line without management approval.

Lethal force. Using a firearm, striking the head with a baton, choking, hitting someone with a car.

Letter of Agent status. Formal, written verification that someone is acting as an agent of the owner in respect to enforcing the Trespass to Property Act or Criminal Code on, or in relation to, the property.

Mall conduct cards. Small cards pre-approved by mall management that clarify expected conduct of patrons while on mall property

Mob. A group of like-minded individuals assembled for an unlawful purpose.

Modus operandi. The way in which someone performs a task or action.

Motive. Reason to steal (e.g., resentment for being passed over for promotion, being overburdened by debt).

Normal user. Person(s) whom you desire to be in a certain space.

Observers. Those persons who have to be in a certain space to support the "human function" (i.e., someone sitting on her front porch watching the street).

Officer presence. The uniform of the officer establishes an initial display of authority.

Opportunity. Absence of barriers that prevent someone from stealing.

Order maintenance patrol. A patrol conducted by two or more Security Officers to enforce the Trespass to Property Act in relation to specific prohibited activity on or in relation to a client property.

Private security. The security sector is an essential component in crime prevention, investigation, and protection of all people, assets, and property. It involves all those who have an interest in, a concern for, and are beneficiaries of security. It is both a provider of security services and security goods (equipment). It includes all the stakeholders: owners, employees, and organized labour; governments, corporations, and businesses; educators, standards organizations, and associations. It is both dedicated (in-house) and for hire (contract).

Risk. Anything that could hurt profit. Risk is determined based on an assessment of the criticality, vulnerability, and probability of an incident happening.

Shoulder shift. A spontaneous shrugging of a subject's shoulders. This can be a pre-attack cue.

Slip and fall. Refers to any accident that occurs to a patron resulting in his or her falling on the property.

Tactical communications. Using your voice to persuade/influence the subject.

Thousand-yard stare. A subject's gaze goes blank and he or she appears to be looking right through you. It can be a pre-attack cue.

Timed clock round patrol. A patrol that has specific locations that must be visited by security. A magnetic bar or some other identifier is affixed to each location. The Security Officer carries a device that records his or her visit to the location.

Total survival. The physical, psychological, emotional, and professional survival of an officer.

Wet system. Water remains in the pipes under pressure right at the sprinkler head. These systems can only be used in areas where the temperature remains above freezing.

ENDNOTES

Chapter 1

1. Schnabolk, Charles. 1983. *Physical Security: Practices and Technology*. Stoneham, MA: Butterworth Publishers, 2.
2. Ibid.
3. Ibid., 3.
4. Ibid.
5. Criminal Code of Canada, Section 129 (b).
6. Schnabolk, 3.
7. Ibid.
8. Ibid.
9. Ibid.
10. Ibid.
11. Ibid., 4.
12. Gerden, Robert. 1998. *Private Security: A Canadian Perspective*. Scarborough, ON: Prentice Hall Canada, 18.
13. Schnabolk, 5.
14. Ibid.
15. Ibid., 7.
16. Ibid.
17. Ibid.
18. Ibid., 11.
19. Ibid., 12.
20. Ibid.
21. Ibid.
22. Ibid., 17.
23. Ibid.
24. Ibid., 18.
25. Ibid.

Chapter 2

1. Mckoy, Heath Jon. 1999. Private security puts public at risk, police say. *Southam Newspapers*. December.
2. Ibid.
3. Ibid.
4. Gerden, Robert. 1998. *Private Security: A Canadian Perspective*. Scarborough, ON: Prentice Hall Canada, 24.
5. Ibid.

Chapter 3

1. Nowicki, Ed. 1996. *Total Survival*. Powers Lake, WI: Performance Dimensions Publishing, Introduction, vii.
2. Ibid.
3. Ibid., 7.
4. Ibid., 5.

5. Remsberg, Charles. 1993. *The Tactical Edge: Surviving High Risk Patrol*. Northbrooks, IL: Calibre Press, 281.
6. Ibid., 47.
7. Ibid.
8. Ibid., 55.
9. Ibid.
10. Ibid., 156.

Chapter 4
1. Nowicki, Ed. 1996. *Total Survival.* Powers Lake, WI: Performance Dimensions Publishing, 24–26.

Chapter 13
1. Williams, Timothy. 1997. *Protection of Assets Manual*. Santa Monica, CA: Merritt, 41.
2. Ibid., 2.
3. Ibid., 3.
4. Ibid., 26.
5. Ibid., 29.
6. Ibid., 25.
7. Ibid., 11.
8. Ibid.
9. Ibid., 21.
10. Ibid.
11. Ibid., 21–22.

Chapter 17
1. Williams, Timothy. 1997. *Protection of Assets Manual*. Santa Monica, CA: Merritt Publishing, 9.
2. Ibid., 10.

Chapter 19
1. *Merriam-Webster's Collegiate Dictionary*. 10th ed. 1996. Springfield, MA: Merriam-Webster.
2. Kingsbury, Arthur. 1999. Functions of the Crime Prevention Officer. In *Handbook of Loss Prevention and Crime Prevention*, 3rd ed., by Lawrence J. Fennelly. Toronto, ON: Butterworth-Heinemann, 4.
3. Fennelly, Lawrence J. 1999. *Handbook of Loss Prevention and Crime Prevention*. 3rd ed. Toronto, ON: Butterworth-Heinemann, 10.
4. Ibid., 5.
5. Ibid., 8.
6. Ibid., 14.
7. Jeffrey, C.R. 1977. *Crime Prevention Through Environmental Design*. 2nd ed. Beverly Hills, CA: Sage Publications.
8. Sorensen, Severin, et al. 1998. *Crime Prevention Through Environmental Design in Public Housing*. Bethesda, MD: Sparta Consulting Corporation, 2-7 to 2-8.
9. Crowe, Timothy. 2000. *Crime Prevention Through Environmental Design*. 2nd ed. Boston, MA: Butterworth-Heineman, 36.
10. Ibid., 37.
11. Ibid., 51.
12. Ibid., 39.
13. Ibid., 39–40.

BIBLIOGRAPHY

Books

Crowe, Timothy. 2000. *Crime Prevention Through Environmental Design*. 2nd ed. Boston, MA: Butterworth-Heineman.

Fay, John J. 1993. *Encyclopaedia of Security Management*. Boston, MA: Butterworth-Heinemann.

Fennelly, Lawrence J. 1999. *Handbook of Loss Prevention and Crime Prevention*. 3rd ed. Toronto, ON: Butterworth-Heinemann.

Gerden, Robert. 1998. *Private Security: A Canadian Perspective*. Scarborough, ON: Prentice Hall Canada.

Groot, Norman. 1998. *Legal Liability of the Canadian Private Investigator*. North York, ON: Andijk Incorporated.

Jeffrey, C.R. 1977. *Crime Prevention Through Environmental Design*. 2nd ed. Beverly Hills, CA: Sage Publications.

Nowicki, Ed. 1996. *Total Survival*. Powers Lake, WI: Performance Dimensions Publishing.

Remsberg, Charles. 1993. *The Tactical Edge: Surviving High Risk Patrol*. Northbrooks, IL: Calibre Press.

Rodrigues, Gary. 1998. *The Police Officers Manual*. 15th ed. Toronto, ON: Thomson Canada Limited.

Salhany, Roger. 1998. *The Police Manual of Arrest, Seizure & Interrogation*. 6th ed. Toronto, ON: Thomson Canada Limited.

Schnabolk, Charles. 1983. *Physical Security: Practices and Technology*. Stoneham, MA: Butterworth Publishers.

Sorensen, Severin L., Ellen Walsh, and Marina Myhre. 1998. *Crime Prevention Through Environmental Design in Public Housing*. Bethesda, MD: Sparta Consulting Corporation.

Williams, Timothy. 1997. *Protection of Assets Manual*. Santa Monica, CA: Merritt Publishing.

Internet Resources

Crime Prevention and Security Links Page. Australain Centre for Security Research (ACSR) <security.macarthur.uws.edu.au/links.htm>

McKay, Tom. 1997. CPTED Case Study: Council Ring Plaza. Rev. November. <www.peelpolice.on.ca/council.html>

Smith, Mary S. 1996. Crime Prevention Through Environmental Design in Parking Facilities. NIJ Research in Brief series. April. <www.securitymanagement.com/library/000199.html>

Newspaper Articles

Harrington, Carol. 1999. Police to discuss regulating guards. *The Globe and Mail.* October 25, A6.

Mckoy, Heath Jon. 1999. Private security puts public at risk, police say. *Southam Newspapers.* December.

Smith, Susan. 1999. New "urban village" seeks old-fashioned feel. *The Globe and Mail.* October 22.

Periodical Articles

Connor, Greg. 1992. Improving officer perception. *LAW and ORDER magazine.* March. Vol. 40, no. 3, 39–40.

Dykes, Coulbourn M. and Major Edward L. Guthrie. 1992. Accreditation accrues benefits. *LAW and ORDER magazine.* March. Vol. 40, no. 3, 116.

Kingsbury, Arthur. 1999. Functions of the Crime Prevention Officer. In *Handbook of Loss Prevention and Crime Prevention*, 3rd ed., by Lawrence J. Fennelly. Toronto, ON: Butterworth-Heinemann.

Lavell, Loretta. 1999. Safeguard your garden through environmental design. *Plant & Garden.* Feb/March.

Longmore-Etheridge, Ann. 1999. The high stakes of child safety. *Security Management.* October.

Lopez, Carl H. 1992. The will to survive. *LAW and ORDER magazine.* March. Vol. 40, no. 3., 29–30.

McKay, Tom. 1998. Empty spaces, dangerous places. *Plan Canada.* January.

———. 1998. Redesigning the interior of the Kitchener Public Library. *Problem Solving Quarterly.* Summer.

———. 1998. School's redesign improves safety, wins award. *School Safety.* Spring.

Morrison, Richard. 1992. You survived the street, now can you survive cross-examination? *LAW and ORDER magazine.* March. Vol. 40, no. 3., 86–88.

Noose, Gregory. 1992. Basic investigative interviewing skills. *LAW and ORDER magazine.* March. Vol. 40, no. 3., 101–107.

Okoszko, Lester. 1994. Edged weapons defensive training. *LAW and ORDER magazine.* March. Vol. 42, no. 3, 25–26.

Reports

Linden, Rick, Dr. 1994. *Crime and Incident Analysis for Community Policing.* Toronto, ON: Ministry of Supply and Services.

INDEX